GRIEF SHARE®
Your Journey from Mourning to Joy

WELCOME TO GRIEFSHARE: WHAT TO EXPECT

You are to be commended for taking the step of coming to this GriefShare group. In the weeks to come, you'll discover how helpful it is to be around people who have an understanding of how you feel. These people will accept where you're at in your grief and will offer encouragement and support in the days to come.

Q: IT'S MY FIRST TIME AT GRIEFSHARE. WHAT'S GOING TO HAPPEN?

A: You'll view a weekly video seminar on a grief-related topic. The videos feature respected counselors and teachers who have faced their own grief and who share insights on how to walk through grief in a healthy manner. There are also personal testimonies of people who share their struggles and what has helped them. After the video, you'll spend time as a small group discussing the concepts on the video and how they apply to your day-to-day struggles and your life. The discussion time is moderated by your GriefShare leader.

Q: I'M VERY NERVOUS ABOUT BEING HERE. IS THIS NORMAL?

A: Yes. You are not the only one feeling this way right now. Most of the people in your group probably feel the same way (or did the first time they came). Despite your nerves, we encourage you to commit to attending for at least three weeks; that will give you time to make a good decision about whether this group will help you. Other people have shared that the comfort, support, and healing found in this group far outweigh the initial anxiousness.

Q: WILL I HAVE TO TALK DURING THE GROUP?

A: No. The decision to share is yours. You will benefit by just listening to the videos and the discussion. Your group facilitator will encourage you to share when you are ready because not only will sharing help you, your insights might also help someone else.

Q: WHY DO I NEED THIS WORKBOOK?

A: You'll use the video outline to take notes during the videos. Then, during the week you'll find short, daily exercises to help you sort through your emotions and your personal situation and to help you find comfort and answers to your questions. The workbook is a valuable part of your healing process.

Q: I'M NOT A CHRISTIAN. WILL GRIEFSHARE HELP ME?

A: Yes. We want you to feel welcome no matter what your spiritual beliefs are. People from all belief systems (and people who do not practice a faith) tell us that even though they are not Christians, they have found their GriefShare groups to be wonderfully beneficial. So, although our teaching is based out of the Christian Bible and our counsel is what we call "Christ-centered," we recognize and appreciate that not everyone has that viewpoint. We think you'll feel comfortable and that GriefShare will be helpful.

Q: DO I NEED TO HAVE A BIBLE?

A: While you don't need a Bible, since the Bible verses are written out in your workbook and on the video, we do encourage you to talk with your GriefShare leader about getting a Bible of your own. Then you'll be able to look up the verses for yourself, discover the context of the passages, and learn more about what God has to say about your situation.

ABOUT GRIEFSHARE

GriefShare is a network of thousands of grief recovery support groups meeting around the world. GriefShare is a program with direction and purpose. With GriefShare you will learn how to walk the journey of grief and be supported on the way. It is a place where grieving people find healing and hope.

David and Nancy Guthrie, cohosts of the GriefShare videos, have faced the deaths of two of their three children and now minister to others in grief. David and Nancy share what they've learned through the Respite Retreats they hold for couples who have lost children, through speaking around the country, and through their books, including *When Your Family's Lost a Loved One*. Nancy has authored several books, including *Holding On to Hope*, *The One Year Book of Hope*, and *Hearing Jesus Speak into Your Sorrow*. David, Nancy, and their son, Matt, live in Nashville, Tennessee.

HELP FOR HURTING PEOPLE

Listed below is information about other care group resources from Church Initiative, which publishes GriefShare. For further information, call **800-395-5755** (US and Canada) or **919-562-2112** (local and international), visit our website at ***www.churchinitiative.org***, or email us at ***info@churchinitiative.org***.

www.singleandparenting.org
Single & Parenting addresses the unique challenges faced by single parents, whether widowed, divorced, or never-married, offering practical parenting tips and support.

www.divorcecare.org
DivorceCare is a seminar/ small group resource to help people who are hurting because of separation and divorce.

www.dc4k.org
DivorceCare for Kids is designed to bring healing to children of divorce and to give them hope and the tools to develop healthier relationships within their own families.

CONTENTS

How GriefShare Works vii

Group Guidelines ix

GriefShare Resource Center x

God, What Is Going On? xii

Viewer's Guide to the GriefShare Videos xvi

GriefShare Video Experts xvii

GriefShare Sessions*

Session 1   **Is This Normal?** 1
Article: Common Responses to the Death of a Loved One 4

Session 2   **Challenges of Grief** 11

Session 3   **The Journey of Grief – Part One** 21
Article: How to Write a Grief Letter 24

Session 4   **The Journey of Grief – Part Two** 31
Article: How to Ask For and Accept Help 34

Session 5   **Grief and Your Relationships** 43
Article: Caring for Grieving Children 46
Article: Being Honest with Your Comforters 47

Session 6   **Why?** 55

Session 7   **Guilt and Anger** 63
Article: Why Should I Forgive? 66

Session 8   **Complicating Factors** 75
Article: Post-traumatic Stress Disorder 78

Session 9   **Stuck** 85

Session 10   **Lessons of Grief – Part One** 93
Article: Coping with Grief During the Holiday Season 96

Session 11   **Lessons of Grief – Part Two** 103

Session 12   **Heaven** **111**
  Article: God's Forgiveness: An Unlikely Source of Joy and Comfort 114

Session 13   **What Do I Live for Now?** **121**
  Excerpt: Will Life Return to Normal? 125

What's Next? 132

Thank You and Invitation Cards . . . . Back

Care Cards . . . . Back

* Each session includes a note-taking outline for the video, daily **From Mourning to Joy** exercises, and a **My Weekly Grief Work** page.

HOW GRIEFSHARE WORKS

Your GriefShare experience includes three key elements that work together to help you recover from the deep hurt of loss. We encourage you to commit to taking part in all three aspects of GriefShare.

Video seminar – Helpful information on grief-related topics
Group discussion – Facilitated small group discussion time
Personal workbook – Individual study and application of concepts

VIDEO

At each session you'll view a video featuring insights from Christian experts, personal stories of people grieving a death, and dramatic reenactments to help you through the grief process. We encourage you to take notes using the video outlines in your workbook and refer to your notes during the discussion time. The videos average 40 minutes in length.

SUPPORT GROUP

After viewing the weekly video, you will participate in a small group discussion about what you saw on the video and how it applies to your life. You'll stay with the same group of people for the thirteen sessions. It's likely you will begin to see the people in your group as "family."

Your leaders will have questions to guide the group discussion, and you'll spend time catching up on the trials and successes experienced by group members between sessions. Sharing your experiences will help you organize and clarify your thoughts on what is happening to you and allow others to understand how they can help you along your grief journey.

Each week your group will also discuss the daily **From Mourning to Joy** workbook exercises and how they have helped throughout the week.

WORKBOOK-BASED PERSONAL STUDY AND REFLECTION

FROM MOURNING TO JOY EXERCISES: Completing the short daily questions and reading the insights and Bible verses can make a real difference in your recovery.

MY WEEKLY GRIEF WORK: Each week this page offers a personal checkup, a practical "How to" section to help you do your grief work, and journaling prompts. We encourage you to get a separate notebook for journaling, a tremendous help in processing your grief.

NOTE-TAKING OUTLINES: Use these video outlines to take notes while viewing the video seminars.

CARE CARDS: Tear out a perforated Care Card each week and place it where you will see it often throughout each day. Another suggestion is to tear out the cards, laminate them, and put them on a key ring.

GOD, WHAT IS GOING ON? Death reminds us that there is something terribly wrong with the world. Find out what it is and what God is doing to fix it.

HELPFUL ARTICLES: These articles offer practical information on common responses in grief, how to write a grief letter, how to ask for help, how to care for grieving children, the struggle to forgive, coping with grief during holidays and special days, how forgiveness can be a source of comfort, and more.

THANK YOU AND INVITATION CARDS: Fill out and send these perforated postcards to friends and/or your church leaders.

GRIEFSHARE RESOURCE CENTER: Find even more GriefShare resources, available both online and in print, including free daily email encouragements you can sign up for.

If you're active in a church, turn there for support during this difficult time. If you're not, you are missing out on a key element to your healing. Your group leaders can explain how connecting with a church can become an important part of your healing process. God doesn't expect you to carry the whole load by yourself. He uses the church and the people in it to help in your recovery.

We've seen GriefShare help people in grief heal and develop hope for the future. We encourage you to become committed to your GriefShare group and to look expectantly at what God can do in your life!

GROUP GUIDELINES

Your group will develop its own guidelines, but here are broad suggestions about how to be an effective group member.

SHARE
There is no requirement that you talk or share in the group, but you are encouraged to do so!

LISTEN
Be willing to listen. When someone else is speaking, focus on what that person is saying in order to learn, comfort, and help. Good listening builds relationships. Remember to refrain from cross talk (talking while someone else is talking).

GIVE AND RECEIVE ADVICE WISELY
The best advice you will get comes from the experts you will see on the GriefShare videos. Remember, the advice you receive from fellow group members may not be appropriate in your circumstances. Be very wise in offering advice, and don't insist that others take that advice or respond to issues in the same way you have.

COMPLETE THE WORKBOOK EXERCISES
Doing the workbook exercises benefits both you and the group. By completing your **From Mourning to Joy** exercises, as well as attending the meetings, you'll be able to get the most out of GriefShare that you can. The exercises also prepare you for the discussion time. Group discussion reaches its full potential when everyone does the exercises.

BE SENSITIVE
Some of you are naturally outgoing and comfortable sharing your feelings. Some of you are a bit shy. If you are outgoing, make sure you don't dominate the group. If you tend to be quiet or shy, make an effort to participate (you'll be glad you did).

DON'T "RANK" LOSSES
You might think that some types of losses are deeper and more profound than others. Grief is personal, and everyone processes it in the context of personal life experiences and perspective. It would not be fair to say that one type of loss should be grieved more deeply than another.

DATING WITHIN THE GROUP
This is a group designed to help you and the other group members heal from the hurt of grief. For that reason, dating is not permitted among group members. If you have lost a spouse, you'll see on the videos that dating too early can add to your hurt. You and the other group members are emotionally vulnerable. It's important to build mutual trust, demonstrating that you are part of this group to find healing.

BE WELL-MANNERED
Take care to protect the integrity of the GriefShare program as well as each group member. Please make every effort to avoid speaking of others in disparaging terms.

MAINTAIN CONFIDENTIALITY
Don't talk about things you hear in the group to people outside the group. This will help develop an atmosphere of trust. (Keep in mind, there is no way the group can guarantee confidentiality, so use discretion about what you share.)

BE TEACHABLE
Everyone in the group comes from different situations and backgrounds. Be respectful of the differences, knowing that group members are there to find hope, comfort, and healing.

MAKE A COMMITMENT
Make a commitment to attend each weekly session and the thirteen-week process. This process is a journey, and finding peace and comfort doesn't happen overnight. It takes time to grow through this painful experience. You may find it helpful to attend two or three thirteen-week cycles before you are ready to move on.

Access your free resources

HELP & DIRECTION
WHEN YOU NEED IT

GRIEFSHARE.ORG/MY

Free online help from GriefShare

View the GriefShare session videos
Watch again or catch up on those you missed.

 Activate your daily emails
Sign up for "A Season of Grief," 365 days of encouragement.

 Discover bonus content
View bonus videos from your favorite experts and personal stories.

 Access classic videos
See the entire past edition of GriefShare.

Get holiday help
Find tips to help you through the Thanksgiving and Christmas season.

More help is available!

GRIEFSHARE.ORG/MY

Watch GriefShare videos online—for free

CATCH UP, GET AHEAD, OR REVIEW

GRIEFSHARE.ORG/MY

Access session videos online

You can watch the very same GriefShare videos you see during GriefShare meetings, in your home. It's a great way to:

- Catch up if you miss a meeting
- Watch a video before your session begins
- Review a video you've already seen

And much more ...

See additional bonus videos from previous editions of GriefShare for free.

How to watch?

GRIEFSHARE.ORG/MY

Need help? Talk to your GriefShare leader!

GOD, WHAT IS GOING ON?

It's not fair that my sister was killed by a drunk driver. She was so young.
My husband was getting ready to retire. Why did he have to suffer and die from cancer?
Why did God allow my child to be murdered?

DOES GOD CARE ABOUT YOUR PAIN?

It's a fair question. Does God really understand what you are going through after your loss?

In the Bible, you'll find assurance that God does understand and wants to help you:

 He is described as *"the Father of compassion and the God of all comfort"* (2 Corinthians 1:3).

 He knows what is happening to you: *"But you, God, see the trouble of the afflicted; you consider their grief and take it in hand"* (Psalm 10:14a).

 God wants you to talk about your hurts, to *"pour out your heart to him"* (Psalm 62:8 NLT).

Do you see? He hears your cries for help and He invites you to come to Him for comfort.

GOD'S PLAN TO END YOUR SUFFERING

Not only does God want to ease your suffering, He actually relates to it. How can God understand a human problem like grief? He can relate because He grieved the unjust execution of His Son, Jesus.

As painful as it was, God allowed Jesus to die as part of His plan to end suffering and death. He wanted to bring comfort, hope, and healing to you. But to appreciate this plan, you have to understand the reason suffering and death exist.

THE REASON WE SUFFER

All of us have disobeyed God. This is not a new problem. It stretches all the way back to Adam and Eve.

The Bible calls this disobedience *"sin"* and describes its ultimate consequence:

 "All have sinned and fall short of the glory of God." (Romans 3:23)

 "The wages of sin is death." (Romans 6:23a)

This creates a seemingly hopeless future for us:

 Because God is pure and holy, He cannot tolerate sin.

He punishes sin. It's the only possible response consistent with His righteous character.

 The penalty for our sin is suffering in this life and physical death followed by eternal punishment.

THE REASON YOU CAN HAVE HOPE

Even in His holiness, God is compassionate. He does not want us to meet our deserved fate. The Bible describes another side of God's character, one that should encourage you:

 "God is love." (1 John 4:8b)

 He is patient with us: *"The LORD is compassionate and gracious, slow to anger, abounding in love"* (Psalm 103:8).

 He is *"rich in mercy"* (Ephesians 2:4).

God's love and mercy are so deep that He wants to rescue each of us from the consequences of our disobedience (sin). He sent His only Son, Jesus Christ, to die on the cross to pay the penalty for that sin. Jesus experienced death and separation from God, on our behalf, even though He was perfect. It is the ultimate expression of God's love:

 "For God so loved the world that he gave his one and only Son, that whoever believes in him shall not perish but have eternal life." (John 3:16)

CLAIMING GOD'S HOPE FOR YOUR LIFE

Ultimately God's plan will put an end to murder, cancer, tragic accidents, loneliness, sadness, depression, and grief. One day *"there will be no more death or mourning or crying or pain"* (Revelation 21:4). So even in the sorrow you feel right now, you can look forward with hope to the fulfillment of this plan.

But to benefit from God's plan, you have to let Him know that you want to be an active part of it.

This involves agreeing that you disobey God and that you need Christ to die in your place to save you from experiencing the full penalty of your sin (eternal punishment and separation from God).

THIS ISN'T VERY COMFORTING

Right about now, you may feel a bit beat-up or perhaps offended that God views you as a sinner. We get that. These truths are tough to process on a good day, even harder when you're dealing with grief. Quite frankly, that's why it's easier to rest in the illusion that sources outside our control are the cause of the problems we face.

But if we're honest, we have to admit that murderers, terrorists, and white-collar criminals aren't the only ones causing suffering in this world. Think about it:

 Have you ever lost your temper and said things that hurt someone?

Was there a time when you slacked off on your responsibilities and caused work to pile up on someone else?

 Have you ever held a grudge that caused you to withhold kindness?

 Was there ever a time when you took pleasure in sharing gossip that hurt someone's reputation?

And while those acts (or others like them) are small when compared to the big evils of the world, anything you do that God doesn't like is sin, and the punishment is eternal suffering. That's why it's critical to share these truths with you now, even in the midst of your grief. Your eternal destiny is at stake.

HOPE FOR FORGIVENESS AND HEALING

Thankfully the Bible says, *"If you declare with your mouth, 'Jesus is Lord,' and believe in your heart that God raised him from the dead, you will be saved"* (Romans 10:9). In other words, you'll be spared from eternal suffering and separation from God. And, one day, you'll get to see what life is like in a perfect world that's free of sin and suffering for eternity.

If you have never confessed your need for a savior, you can do it now by praying something like this:

Dear Jesus,

I am grieving, and I need Your help. I know that I am a sinner and that my sin has separated me from You. But I believe that You experienced the punishment that should have been mine by dying on the cross for my sins. I believe You rose from the dead so I could have the hope of living forever with You instead of spending eternity separated from You. Thank you for enduring the grief and the pain to show Your love for me. I place my trust in You to help me heal.

Amen

THINGS REALLY ARE DIFFERENT NOW

If you've come to believe what the words of that prayer expressed, many things have changed. Look at some of the remarkable and comforting things that have occurred:

 You know what's going on: While you may never know all the details concerning why your loved one died (Deuteronomy 29:29), you have a better idea of the big picture: we live in a sin-cursed world and God is doing something about it. Your suffering only makes sense in the context of that story. But now that you believe in Christ, the best thing is that you'll see and enjoy the culmination of His plan to rid the world of sin and suffering.

 You have a relationship with the God of all comfort: Believing in Christ for the forgiveness of sins and the promise of eternal life in Him is essential to your healing. It allows you to have a personal relationship with the God of all comfort. God loved you enough to go through the death of His Son for you. He is familiar with your suffering and will walk with you through the toughest days of your grief journey, offering comfort for today and hope for the future.

- **You have reason for hope:** There's more to life than this world. Jesus promised to gather all who trusted Him for salvation into an eternal paradise. There will be no more tears, suffering, or death in that place. Rest your hope on this unshakable promise. Doing so will transform the way you grieve. *"And now, dear brothers and sisters, we want you to know what will happen to the believers who have died so you will not grieve like people who have no hope."* (1 Thessalonians 4:13 NLT)

- **God will use your suffering for good:** God promises to use all your experiences (good and bad) to help you become more like His Son (Romans 8:28–29). As you grow in your understanding of how wonderful Jesus is, this promise will become increasingly attractive and precious to you.

- **Your sins were forgiven:** *"He is so rich in kindness and grace that he purchased our freedom with the blood of his Son and forgave our sins."* (Ephesians 1:7 NLT)

- **You no longer have to fear being judged by God (Romans 8:1):** And no matter how intense and painful your grief becomes, you can always take solace in the fact that God has lovingly and generously addressed your most pressing need—your need for forgiveness.

- **You received the gift of eternal life:** While we will all experience physical death, Jesus promised that those who believe in Him will never cease to exist. For you have inherited what Jesus calls eternal life (John 3:16).

- **You can access God's peace:** *"Do not be anxious about anything, but in every situation, by prayer and petition, with thanksgiving, present your requests to God. And the peace of God, which transcends all understanding, will guard your hearts and your minds in Christ Jesus."* (Philippians 4:6–7)

"He saved us, not because of the righteous things we had done, but because of his mercy. He washed away our sins, giving us a new birth and new life ... Because of his grace he declared us righteous and gave us confidence that we will inherit eternal life." (Titus 3:5–7 NLT)

WHAT'S NEXT?

Turning control of your life over to Jesus is only the first step in an exciting relationship with God. You'll want to get to know Him better and learn His plan for your life. To do this, make time to read the Bible and talk with God about what you're reading. The **From Mourning to Joy** exercises in this workbook can help you get started.

It's also important for you to spend time with people who can help you know Jesus in an even deeper and more intimate way. The best way to do this is to become part of a church that will teach you and guide you in a growing relationship with Jesus. Be sure to tell your GriefShare leader about your decision to follow Christ.

VIEWER'S GUIDE TO THE GRIEFSHARE VIDEOS

The GriefShare videos feature in-depth interviews with leading experts on grief recovery topics. All of these people are deeply committed to helping you heal. You'll find biographical information about each of the video experts on the following pages.

EXPERTS TIMELINE

You are viewing the third edition of the GriefShare videos. Much of the video on this release is fresh, recorded specifically for this edition. But we didn't want you to miss out on some of the most-loved video clips from previous versions of GriefShare, so we have included what we call *"GriefShare Classic"* clips as well.

How will you recognize a *Classic* video clip? Here are some things to watch for:

| Fashions and hairstyles have changed. | Video resolution is lower than current technology. | You'll see video clips showing a younger version of one of our current experts. |

Most importantly, when you see a GriefShare Classic clip, you should pay even more attention to what's being said because it's one of the most helpful and popular video clips from earlier editions of GriefShare. The information is valuable and timeless, even when the styles have changed!

GRIEFSHARE VIDEO EXPERTS

You'll meet these people on the GriefShare videos in the coming weeks. They are experts on grief recovery topics, sharing insights they have learned through years of counseling, teaching, and pastoring, and through their personal experiences of grief.

Sabrina D. Black, author and speaker, is the CEO and clinical director of Abundant Life Counseling Center. She is a limited licensed professional counselor, certified addictions counselor, and certified biblical counselor. She experienced the death of multiple close relatives and the miscarriage of her baby. *www.abundantlifecounseling.webs.com*

Judy Blore was the director of BASIS, a ministry of Handi*Vangelism, for over twenty-two years, providing help for bereaved parents and their families in southeastern Pennsylvania. Judy experienced the death of her mother.

Dave Branon is an editor, a contributor to *Our Daily Bread*, and the author of many devotional articles and books. His book *Beyond the Valley* details his journey after the death of his seventeen-year-old daughter Melissa.

The late **Dr. Bill Bright** was the founder and president of Campus Crusade for Christ. For over fifty years he dedicated his life to helping people find new life and hope through a relationship with Christ.

David Bueno Martin is a bilingual counselor and supervisor at Martin Counseling in Katy, Texas. He also speaks at workshops and seminars. David experienced the loss of a child. *www.martincounseling.com*

Cindy Bultema is a Bible teacher and speaker. She shares her personal testimony in the DVD presentation *He Loves Me*. Cindy has experienced addiction and the death of her fiancé. *www.cindybultema.com*

Michael Card is a Bible teacher, musician, and author. He has recorded over thirty albums and authored/coauthored over twenty-four books, including *A Sacred Sorrow*. His best friend died. *www.michaelcard.com*

Carol Cornish is a counselor and teacher. She is the author of *The Undistracted Widow: Living for God after Losing Your Husband*. Carol is a regular speaker at seminars, workshops, and retreats. Her husband died of cancer.

Dr. Larry Crabb is a psychologist, conference and seminar speaker, Bible teacher, and author. He is the founder of New Way Ministries. His books include *Shattered Dreams*, *Finding God*, and *The Safest Place on Earth*. He experienced the death of his brother in a plane crash.
www.newwayministries.org

Zoricelis Davila is a bilingual counselor and speaker. She has authored several Spanish books, including *¡No sé lo que me pasa!* [*I Don't Know What Is Wrong with Me!*]. Her dad died of cancer.

Dr. Robert DeVries is professor emeritus of church education at Calvin Theological Seminary. His first wife of twenty-eight years died of cancer. Now remarried to **Dr. Susan Zonnebelt-Smeenge**, they work together to help people in grief and are coauthors of many books, including *The Empty Chair: Handling Grief on Holidays and Special Occasions* and *From We to Me*.

Joni Eareckson Tada is an author, artist, broadcaster, and the founder and president of Joni and Friends Ministries. Her books and ministry reflect her experience of God's love and grace since becoming a quadriplegic in a diving accident years ago. She has written over fifty books, including *Heaven* and *When God Weeps*. *www.joniandfriends.org*

Sandy Elder is a biblical counselor with a master's degree in religion from Westminster Theological Seminary. She presently counsels at New Life Presbyterian Church in Dresher, Pennsylvania, and has counseled five years with the Christian Counseling and Educational Foundation in Glenside, Pennsylvania. She experienced the death of her parents.

Dr. Michael R. Emlet is a counselor at the Christian Counseling and Educational Foundation (CCEF) in Glenside, Pennsylvania. Before joining CCEF, he worked as a family physician for twelve years. He has authored *Angry Children* (a booklet) and *CrossTalk: Where Life & Scripture Meet*. *www.ccef.org*

Elyse Fitzpatrick is a counselor and the director of Women Helping Women Ministries. She has authored/coauthored many books, including *A Steadfast Heart: Experiencing God's Comfort in Life's Storms* and *Overcoming Fear, Worry, and Anxiety*.
www.elysefitzpatrick.com

Julie Ganschow is a counselor and teacher at Reigning Grace Counseling Center in Kansas City, Missouri. She has authored several books, including *Seeing Depression Through the Eyes of Grace*. She maintains a daily blog on counseling issues. Julie experienced the loss of her mother.
www.biblicalcounselingforwomen.org

Ruth Graham is a speaker and Bible teacher. She is the founder and president of Ruth Graham Ministries. Her books include *In Every Pew Sits a Broken Heart* and *Fear Not Tomorrow, God Is Already There*. Her mother passed away.
www.ruthgrahamministries.org

Anne Graham Lotz is a speaker and the president of AnGeL Ministries. She hosts revivals and conferences across the United States. Her books include *Why? Trusting God When You Don't Understand*, *Heaven: My Father's House*, and *The Vision of His Glory*. Her brother-in-law and mother died.
www.annegrahamlotz.com

Brad Hambrick is the pastor of counseling at The Summit Church in Durham, North Carolina. His books include *God's Attributes: Rest for Life's Struggles*. His grandfather passed away. *www.bradhambrick.com*

Hank Hanegraaff is the president and chairman of the board of the Christian Research Institute and hosts the daily radio program *Bible Answer Man*. He has authored over twenty books, including *AfterLife: What You Really Want to Know About Heaven and the Hereafter*. His father died. *www.hankhanegraaff.com*

Dr. Jack Hayford is the founding pastor of The Church on the Way in Van Nuys, California. He has authored/coauthored over 100 books and has written over 600 songs. He is the founder and chancellor of The King's University in Los Angeles. Dr. Hayford experienced the loss of his sister and his parents. *www.jackhayford.org*

The late **Dr. E. V. Hill** was the pastor at Mt. Zion Missionary Baptist Church in Los Angeles for over forty years. Dr. Hill experienced the death of his wife.

Dr. Avak Albert Howsepian is an assistant professor of psychiatry at the University of California, San Francisco-Fresno, Medical Education Program, and a staff psychiatrist in the VA Mental Health Clinic.

The late **Barbara Johnson** was a humorous writer and speaker. Having lost two sons and her husband, she was involved in grief ministry. Her many books include **Laughter from Heaven, Splashes of Joy in the Cesspools of Life**, and **God's Most Precious Jewels Are Crystallized Tears**.

Dr. Robert W. Kellemen is a licensed clinical professional counselor. He is the founder and CEO of RPM Ministries. He has authored several books, including *God's Healing for Life's Losses*. As a young man in seminary, Dr. Kellemen experienced the death of his father. *www.rpmministries.org*

Dr. Crawford Loritts is an author and the senior pastor of Fellowship Bible Church in Roswell, Georgia. He is a frequent speaker for evangelistic outreaches around the world, colleges, professional sports teams, and Christian conferences. His newborn daughter died.

Susan Lutz served as a counselor at the Christian Counseling and Educational Foundation in Glenside, Pennsylvania, for over fifteen years. She now counsels at her church, New Life Presbyterian Church of Dresher. She authored the booklet *Thankfulness: Even When It Hurts.* Her parents passed away.

Dr. Erwin Lutzer is the senior pastor of the Moody Church in Chicago, Illinois. He has written over twenty books, including *One Minute After You Die*, and is the featured speaker on three radio programs heard on Christian stations nationwide. He experienced the loss of his grand-daughter, who was stillborn.

Dr. Elias Moitinho is the director of clinical training and an associate professor of counseling at Liberty University in Lynchburg, Virginia. He has years of experience serving as a pastor, counselor, professor, and the director of a Christian counseling center. His dad died of cancer.

Janet Paschal is a Christian singer and songwriter. She has received Grammy nominations, is a conference speaker, and has been a guest on Christian radio and television talk shows. She has authored *The Good Road* and *Treasures of the Snow*. Janet experienced the loss of her grandfather.
www.janetpaschal.com

Lorraine Peterson, author of *Restore My Soul*, has been a teacher in the United States and in American schools in Ecuador and Mexico. Lorraine currently resides in Mexico, where she ministers to young people and those who have experienced the death of a loved one. Her mother and stepmother both died in car accidents.

Dr. David Powlison is a faculty member at the Christian Counseling and Educational Foundation in Glenside, Pennsylvania. He has been counseling for over thirty years and has authored books, articles, and booklets, including *Healing after Abortion* and *Facing Death with Hope: Living for What Lasts*. www.ccef.org

Lois Rabey is a speaker and writer. She has authored several books, including *When Your Soul Aches* and *Moments for Those Who Have Lost a Loved One*. Lois lost her husband in a hot-air balloon ride accident.

Dr. Robert C. Roberts is a distinguished professor of ethics at Baylor University and received his Ph.D. from Yale University in philosophical theology. He is the author of several articles and books, including *Spiritual Emotions*.

Joyce Rogers, widow of Dr. Adrian Rogers, is a speaker and Bible teacher. She is the author of several books, including *Grace for the Widow* and *Lean Hard on Jesus*.
www.rejoycewithjoycerogers.com

Phil Sasser is the senior pastor of Sovereign Grace Church in Apex, North Carolina, and director of church governance of Sovereign Grace Ministries. He teaches regularly at the Sovereign Grace Ministries Pastors College in Louisville, Kentucky, and has been in ministry for over three decades. His father passed away.

Dr. Joseph Stowell is the president of Cornerstone University in Grand Rapids, Michigan, and previously served as the president of the Moody Bible Institute of Chicago for eighteen years. Dr. Stowell is an internationally recognized speaker and the author of *Eternity*, *The Upside of Down: Finding Hope When It Hurts*, and other books.

Dr. Siang-Yang Tan is a professor of psychology at Fuller Theological Seminary. He has authored many publications, including *Rest* and *Coping with Depression* with John Ortberg. He is the senior pastor of First Evangelical Church Glendale in California. He experienced the death of his father.

Dr. Paul David Tripp is the president of Paul Tripp Ministries and has authored many books, including *Forever* and *A Shelter in the Time of Storm*. He is a professor of pastoral life and care at Redeemer Seminary, Dallas, Texas. Dr. Tripp experienced the death of his father. *www.paultripp.com*

Dr. Stephen Viars is the pastor and a biblical counselor at Faith Baptist Church and Faith Biblical Counseling Ministries in Lafayette, Indiana. He authored *Putting Your Past in Its Place: Moving Forward to Freedom and Forgiveness*. He experienced the sudden death of his father.

Dr. Edward T. Welch is a counselor at the Christian Counseling and Educational Foundation in Glenside, Pennsylvania. His books include *Depression: Looking Up from the Stubborn Darkness* and *When I Am Afraid: A Step-by-Step Guide Away from Fear and Anxiety*. His parents passed away. *www.ccef.org*

James White is the pastor at Christ Our King Community Church in Raleigh, North Carolina. He currently serves as the executive vice president of organizational relations for the YMCA of the Triangle and as a board member for Carver Bible College. James experienced the loss of his parents.

H. Norman Wright is a grief therapist and certified trauma specialist. He is the author of over seventy books, including *Experiencing Grief* and *Recovering from Losses in Life*. He experienced the death of his wife and son. *www.hnormanwright.com*

Ravi Zacharias, president of the Atlanta-based Ravi Zacharias International Ministries, was born in India and immigrated to Canada in 1966. He has written many books, has lectured in more than fifty countries, and hosts weekly radio programs. *www.rzim.org*

The late **Zig Ziglar**, author of *Confessions of a Grieving Christian* and other books, was a motivational speaker and chairman of the Zig Ziglar Corporation. In *Confessions*, he relays the story of his journey through grief after the loss of his daughter.

Dr. Susan Zonnebelt-Smeenge is a licensed clinical psychologist. She lost her husband eighteen years after he was diagnosed with a malignant brain tumor. Now remarried to **Dr. Robert DeVries**, they work together to help people in grief and are joint authors of many books, including *Getting to the Other Side of Grief: Overcoming the Loss of a Spouse* and *Traveling through Grief*.

IS THIS NORMAL?

YOU WAKE UP AND THE GRIEF IS STILL THERE; thirty minutes later you're still at the bathroom sink, toothbrush in hand. You can't remember your coworker's name ... again. Tears come without warning. The knife in your heart twists and turns. Other people just don't get it; they go about their days as if nothing has changed. How long is it going to be like this? *I don't know if I can make it through*, you worry.

As you view this week's video and complete the daily **FROM MOURNING TO JOY** exercises and **MY WEEKLY GRIEF WORK**, you'll begin to see:

- Why your grief experience is harder than you imagined

- Why the intensity and duration of your emotions are normal and appropriate

- Despite how you feel right now, there is reason for hope

VIDEO OUTLINE

Use this outline to write down important concepts, encouraging words, or questions you have while viewing the video.

WHAT IS GRIEF?

Intense and chaotic

"Am I losing my mind?"

Something we hide

A proper response to loss

"God doesn't expect us to put a plastic smile on a broken heart." –Dr. Stephen Viars

Something Jesus did

PERMISSION TO GRIEVE

Honestly express your emotions

Don't suppress your feelings   (Psalm 61:1–2, Matthew 5:4)

Consequences of suppressing grief

THE INTENSITY OF GRIEF

A tangled ball of emotions

The pain won't last   (Ecclesiastes 3:4)

"God values authenticity." –Dr. Stephen Viars

Lean into grief

Postpone big decisions

Do the next thing

Commit to GriefShare   (Ecclesiastes 4:9–10)

In this week's From Mourning to Joy exercises ...
Debi shares honestly about her deep pain after her daughter's death, her struggle to function, and her lack of desire to pray. Each day this week, you'll look at Bible passages addressing these struggles and others you might be facing.

How to watch
session videos online

Log on to **griefshare.org/my** to watch full GriefShare session videos. It's a great option if you:

- Missed a meeting and want to see the video
- Want to rewatch something you saw
- Want to review before your group meeting

Watch the videos today!

GRIEFSHARE.ORG/MY

COMMON RESPONSES TO THE DEATH OF A LOVED ONE

The responses below were shared by people who've faced a loved one's death.
Having an idea of what is normal in grief can be helpful.

You'll likely experience many emotions at once. Grief emotions are not orderly, but are more like a tangled ball. And some of the emotions listed here are polar opposites! Note that this list, while long, is not exhaustive. After looking over this list, if you're not sure if your grief experience is normal, talk with your GriefShare group leader. He or she will be able to help you.

Please understand that thinking you don't want to go on is normal, but thinking about suicide–especially making plans to take your life–is not normal. Seek help immediately.

- ○ Abandoned
- ○ Afraid of facing emotions
- ○ Ambushed by grief
- ○ Anger with others, self, loved one, and/or God
- ○ Anguish
- ○ Annoyance
- ○ Anxiety
- ○ Apathy
- ○ Avoiding church
- ○ Avoiding grief
- ○ Avoiding thinking about the death
- ○ Being harsh with others
- ○ Betrayed
- ○ Bitterness
- ○ Blame
- ○ Can't pray
- ○ Can't talk about loved one
- ○ Change of priorities
- ○ Comparing your grief to other people's
- ○ Compassion
- ○ Complaining
- ○ Concerned about your family members
- ○ Confusion
- ○ Consumed by grief
- ○ Crisis of beliefs
- ○ Crying
- ○ Dazed
- ○ Denial
- ○ Depending on God
- ○ Depression

- ○ Desire for justice
- ○ Despair
- ○ Devastation
- ○ Disappointment
- ○ Disbelief
- ○ Discontentment
- ○ Discouragement
- ○ Disorganized
- ○ Disoriented
- ○ Distracted
- ○ Diving into work
- ○ Don't want to go on
- ○ Drained
- ○ Drawing closer to God
- ○ Dread
- ○ Emotional wreck
- ○ Emptiness
- ○ Encouragement
- ○ Envy
- ○ Exhaustion/weakness
- ○ Fatigue
- ○ Fear of future
- ○ Feeling judged
- ○ Feeling like everything is in slow motion
- ○ Feeling like everything is too hard
- ○ Feeling like God isn't there
- ○ Feeling like mush
- ○ Feeling like something's missing
- ○ Feeling like you're doing something wrong
- ○ Feeling like you're losing your mind

- ○ Feeling like your faith isn't working
- ○ Feeling like your grief is marginalized
- ○ Feeling out of control
- ○ Feeling part of you is gone, ripped away
- ○ Feeling rushed
- ○ Feeling you're being a burden
- ○ Financial worries
- ○ Flashbacks
- ○ Forgetfulness
- ○ Frustration
- ○ Full of questions
- ○ Going through the motions
- ○ Guilt
- ○ Hallucinations
- ○ Happy your loved one is no longer suffering
- ○ Heartbroken
- ○ Heightened emotions
- ○ Helping everyone but yourself
- ○ Helplessness
- ○ Hiding grief
- ○ Hope
- ○ Hopelessness
- ○ Hurt
- ○ Impatience
- ○ In a dark tunnel
- ○ Inability to do things as well as you used to
- ○ Inability to function
- ○ Inadequacy
- ○ Increased appetite
- ○ Insomnia
- ○ Internalizing grief
- ○ Intrusive thoughts
- ○ Irritable
- ○ Isolating self
- ○ Jealousy
- ○ Lack of concentration
- ○ Lack of focus
- ○ Loneliness
- ○ Loss of appetite
- ○ Loss of identity
- ○ Loss of purpose
- ○ Making silly mistakes
- ○ Memory loss
- ○ Mental fog
- ○ Missing loved one
- ○ Nervous
- ○ Nightmares
- ○ No interest in doing things
- ○ No sense of time
- ○ Not allowing self to grieve

- ○ Not enjoying what you used to enjoy
- ○ Not trusting God
- ○ Numbing pain
- ○ Out of control
- ○ Overwhelmed
- ○ Panic attacks
- ○ Peace
- ○ Physical problems: stomachache, headache, chest and heart hurting, nausea, hurting all over, migraines, shortness of breath
- ○ Prayer
- ○ Pretending you're okay
- ○ Questioning your sanity
- ○ Questions about heaven
- ○ Rage
- ○ Refusing joy
- ○ Regret
- ○ Rejection by friends
- ○ Relief
- ○ Roller coaster emotions
- ○ Sadness
- ○ Second-guessing
- ○ Self-pity
- ○ Shame
- ○ Shock
- ○ Shutting down
- ○ Shutting people out
- ○ Sleeping a lot
- ○ Social and relational struggles
- ○ Sorrow
- ○ Squashed
- ○ Staying busy
- ○ Staying in bed
- ○ Stress
- ○ Stuffing down emotions
- ○ Surprise
- ○ Tangled emotions
- ○ Thankfulness
- ○ Tired
- ○ Trying to take care of everything yourself
- ○ Turning to God
- ○ Unable to make decisions
- ○ Uncomfortable with others
- ○ Unproductive
- ○ Unwilling to accept help
- ○ Vindictiveness
- ○ Vulnerable
- ○ Wanting to rush through this
- ○ Worry
- ○ Other _____

FROM MOURNING TO JOY
ENCOURAGEMENT AND COMFORT FROM GOD'S WORD
Session One - Is This Normal?

Every session includes five short, daily exercises. Each day you'll read a Bible passage relevant to the emotions, struggles, and questions grieving people face. Then you'll learn how to apply it to your life and how it is relevant as you seek comfort and healing. At the end of each session is **My Weekly Grief Work**, a tremendous tool with practical steps you can take to aid in healing.

DEBI: "I DIDN'T WANT TO GO ON"

"When I lost my daughter, I didn't want to go on. Life was sucked out of me. I had prayed for healing for her, and this was the way God answered. I couldn't read my Bible. I didn't even pray really. I couldn't do simple things at home. Parents aren't supposed to bury their children. It's supposed to be the other way around. How can I continue to go on?"

Are you hurting? Exhausted? Overwhelmed? Like Debi, do you wonder how you can possibly go on? Maybe you feel that way, but you pretend you're okay. Be assured these are common responses to grief. This week's exercises will help you understand what's typical in grief and how turning to God will help, even when you wonder if God is really here.

DAY 1

I feel like I'm losing my mind
What you are experiencing is normal. It's all part of the grief process. You must go through it in order to heal. But you can make it through.

GOD'S MESSAGE TO YOU
"I am worn out from sobbing. All night I flood my bed with weeping, drenching it with my tears. My vision is blurred by grief." (Psalm 6:6–7a NLT)

1. What does your grief look and feel like?

2. David, the writer of Psalm 6, describes how worn out he is in his grief. Describe your energy level and how it's affecting your daily life.

3. Why do you think attending GriefShare will be helpful?

CONSIDER THIS

"There are no shortcuts to grieving. We're going through the pain in order to heal, because pain does heal."
–Dr. Susan Zonnebelt-Smeenge

"It's like a roller coaster ride. And I hate roller coasters." –Debi

TALKING TO GOD

God, the pain of my grief is pressing in, and sometimes I can't breathe with the force of it. I'm so worn out. Lift me into Your arms. Comfort me with Your presence, and guide me on my journey.

 DAY 2

God, where are You?
What you are experiencing is normal. It's all part of the grief process. You must go through it in order to heal. But you can make it through.

GOD'S MESSAGE TO YOU
"Why, LORD, do you stand far off? Why do you hide yourself in times of trouble?" (Psalm 10:1)

1. Describe your recent feelings about God's presence.

2. If you feel like God is not here, does that mean it's true? Why or why not?

3. Why do you think God wants you to know that godly people of the past felt like He was far off (see Psalm 10:1)?

CONSIDER THIS

"When you're in the middle of grief you don't always sense His presence. So, now what? ...

Keep hurting.
Keep trusting.
Don't quit.

"Say, 'This is where I am. I'm going to accept it. I hate it, but God is somehow at work. I don't feel it, but I'm going to live by faith.'"
–Dr. Larry Crabb

TALKING TO GOD

God, where are You? I need You desperately, but I don't feel like You're near. Despite my feelings, I'm going to keep turning to You because the Bible says You are an ever-present help in times of trouble. You really are here, and You're working even in my darkness.

 DAY 3

Finding stability
"How are you doing?" people ask. You force a smile and lie, "Oh, I'm doing alright."

GOD'S MESSAGE TO YOU
"O God, listen to my cry! Hear my prayer! From the ends of the earth, I cry to you for help when my heart is overwhelmed. Lead me to the towering rock of safety." (Psalm 61:1–2 NLT)

1. At what times do you pretend you have things together?

2. David, a King of Israel, strong both physically and spiritually, is being authentic in his grief in Psalm 61. He's admitting his weaknesses, that he's overwhelmed. When are you most authentic in your grief?

"I remember trying to read my Bible, but there was this white noise in the background." –Carla

3. Why do you think being honest about your grief leads to more stable, secure footing than pretending you're doing okay?

CONSIDER THIS

Authenticity leads to stability.

"I can't understand God as my rock unless I'm willing to acknowledge that I'm feeling overwhelmed. To be able to talk to God and to other people in my life about it is an important step in processing [grief] with truth."
–Dr. Stephen Viars

TALKING TO GOD

God, sometimes it's easier to pretend things are fine, but really, they're not. I'm overwhelmed. I long to feel some security and stability in my life. Lead me to a new place in my relationship with You, a place where I know with certainty that You are my rock.

 DAY 4 **Does prayer really help?**
"When I first walked into this storm of emotions, I walked in constant prayer. It helped me to get out of the storm and start to move forward; it helped me through the questions of why; it helped me through my issues with guilt and regrets." –Hollis

GOD'S MESSAGE TO YOU
"Is anyone among you in trouble? Let them pray." (James 5:13a)

1. Are you facing troubles right now? What does God say to do, according to James 5:13a?

2. How did prayer help Hollis (quoted at the beginning of today's exercise)?

3. Write a prayer to God telling Him what's troubling you today and asking for His help and strength.

We suggest you keep a journal, where you write your honest thoughts and prayers to God. See each session's ***My Weekly Grief Work*** *for journaling ideas.*

CONSIDER THIS

"We don't have to try to protect ourselves, but we can run to Him through prayer and find that He will protect and keep us."
–Elyse Fitzpatrick

TALKING TO GOD

God, You tell me in the Bible that if I'm in trouble, I need to pray. My mind is in a fog a lot of the time these days, but I sure am in trouble without You. Help me to pray.

DAY 5 **It's okay to grieve**
It's okay to grieve. Don't try to keep your tears in check. *"If there were no love, there'd be no grief."* –Zig Ziglar

GOD'S MESSAGE TO YOU
"Jesus wept." (John 11:35)

"So God created mankind in his own image, in the image of God he created them; male and female he created them." (Genesis 1:27)

"Why God? Why?" –Debi

1. Maybe someone has said you should be over your grief by now, or that you're crying too much, or some other judgment. How did Jesus, who is God, who is perfect, grieve the death of His friend Lazarus (see John 11:35)?

2. If you are weeping and grieving because you love someone, you are reflecting God's image; in other words, you're responding the way God would. Write down any worries you've had that there's something wrong with the way you are grieving.

CONSIDER THIS

"It's a very Christlike thing to do, to weep, to grieve. That's exactly how Jesus felt, the Creator of the world, the One who knew He was about to raise Lazarus from the dead, yet Jesus wept."
–Dr. Stephen Viars

TALKING TO GOD

God, the relationship I had with my loved one was one-of-a-kind. When I worry that I'm not grieving the right way, help me understand that I don't need to be anyone but the person You created me to be.

DEBI: LOOKING BACK

"When I look back at when I wanted nothing to do with God, and then I look at my relationship with God now, I know Him in a totally different way. I don't know how life could get any harder than losing your daughter, but God walked with me through that whole time. He didn't let go. He's held me; He's carried me.

"It's not an easy path, but you can make it through. I've been through GriefShare three times, and every time I've gone through it, I've healed even more. It took His Word and a lot of His people surrounding me to help me heal. I'm still healing."

NEXT SESSION
Discover more symptoms of grief and how to start treating them.

GRIEFSHARE MP3 DISC & DOWNLOADABLE AUDIO FILES

Listen to GriefShare wherever you go

Get the full audio track from each of the 13 weekly GriefShare videos on MP3 disc or downloadable audio files. Catch up on sessions you missed or find encouragement by listening to your favorite sessions again.

Order here: griefshare.org/audio

"God never walked away." –Debi

MY WEEKLY GRIEF WORK

Session - One

PERSONAL CHECKUP – TRACK YOUR HEALING PROGRESS
Place a check in the box identifying how you're feeling. Insert words to explain why.

	REALLY BAD	OKAY	PRETTY GOOD	GREAT
EMOTIONALLY				
PHYSICALLY				
SPIRITUALLY				
RELATIONALLY				

JOURNAL TOPICS – MAKING SENSE OF IT ALL
Choose one or more ideas below, or choose your own topic. We encourage
you to use a separate notebook for your weekly journaling.

✏ Pretend you're writing a letter to a friend to help him or her prepare for grief. What would you tell your friend to expect?

✏ Share your fears for the future.

MOVING FORWARD – PRACTICAL STEPS TOWARD HEALING
HOW TO AVOID MAKING A DECISION YOU'LL LATER REGRET
You saw in the video the importance of postponing big decisions.
Before making any major decisions, take the following steps:

1. What decision are you facing?

2. Can this decision wait? Why or why not?

3. List the pros and cons.

4. List people you can speak with about this decision, who will give you wise advice.

5. Write a prayer to God, asking for His direction.

CHALLENGES OF GRIEF

YOU LASH OUT AT A FRIEND BECAUSE SHE KEEPS PUSHING YOU to "move on." You get to the store and realize you don't remember the thirty-minute drive. Scattered thoughts, nausea, rapid heartbeat ... you wonder if you're going crazy.

Rest assured, this is not the case. In this week's video, the daily **FROM MOURNING TO JOY** exercises, and **MY WEEKLY GRIEF WORK**, you'll discover:

 More eye-opening reasons why your pain is so overwhelming

 Some of the overlooked, yet common, effects grief has on your mind, body, and spirit

 How to get things done when you don't feel like you have any energy

VIDEO OUTLINE

Use this outline to write down important concepts, encouraging words, or questions you have while viewing the video.

WHAT'S GOING ON?

"I'm depressed"

"I don't feel like working"

"I'm afraid"

"I'm overwhelmed"

"Deliberately have some grief time." –Judy Blore

"Why do I miss him so?"

Regret   (Luke 16:19–31)

"Are physical symptoms normal?"

Are Physical Symptoms Normal?

Go to the doctor

"My faith isn't working"   (Psalm 143:7–8a, Philippians 4:19, Psalm 23:4)

"God promises to walk with us through the valley." –Brad Hambrick

In this week's From Mourning to Joy exercises ...

Mike shares how he let his emotions rule his life, but finally realized where to find real comfort amid the madness of grief.

"Grief blocks my ability to see God, but I shouldn't conclude that means He is absent." –Dr. Paul David Tripp

MIKE: "YOUR BRAIN STOPS WORKING"

"I was surprised at how intense grief was. You feel like you're going crazy. Your emotions take over and your brain stops working. I was trying to make everybody feel like I was doing good, and then I'd get home and sit there and I'd cry. It was like, 'What do I do now?'"

You can probably relate to what Mike is saying, but at the same time, you realize your grief is uniquely your own; no one will experience it exactly like you. The same is true for your experience of comfort: what is comforting to you might not be comforting to other people. This week you'll learn more about what's normal in grief and how to find comfort that works for you.

DAY 1

Grief affects everything

Is there any area of your life that grief hasn't touched? So what's normal and what can you do about it?

GOD'S MESSAGE TO YOU

"Be merciful to me, LORD, for I am in distress; my eyes grow weak with sorrow, my soul and body with grief. My life is consumed by anguish and my years by groaning; my strength fails because of my affliction, and my bones grow weak." (Psalm 31:9–10)

1. What symptoms of grief is David, the writer of Psalm 31:9–10, experiencing?

2. What does David do in the midst of these grief symptoms?

3. What physical problems have you had as a result of your grief?

4. How has your grief affected your job performance or other duties you have?

"You go into a stupor, and you forget all the promises God's made." –Mike

CONSIDER THIS

"Grief is such chaos. So expect chaos, and then plan for it." –Judy Blore

Make an appointment to see your doctor. It's important to monitor your health during grief.

TALKING TO GOD

God, my mind is mush. I don't feel well physically. I feel uncomfortable relating to my family and even my closest friends. Part of me doesn't care. But I do care, God. Please give me Your strength to make it one step at a time. Help me.

DAY 2 — Your grief is unique

Is something wrong if you don't express your grief the same way others do?

"There's no right way to do this." –Phil Sasser

GOD'S MESSAGE TO YOU

"The king was overcome with emotion. He went up to the room over the gateway and burst into tears. And as he went, he cried, 'O my son Absalom! ... If only I had died instead of you!'" (2 Samuel 18:33a NLT)

"Job stood up and tore his robe in grief. Then he shaved his head and fell to the ground to worship." (Job 1:20 NLT)

"When Jesus saw her weeping ... he was deeply moved in spirit and troubled." (John 11:33)

1. In looking at today's Bible passages, what are the responses of each of the three men?

2. How do you express your grief differently from other people you know? Share any concerns you have about this.

3. The Bible is a way God communicates with us. Why do you think God gives us examples of people grieving differently?

CONSIDER THIS

"Be mindful that what's worked for you won't work for everyone else." –Sabrina D. Black

"You go through at your own timing and pace." –Zoricelis Davila

TALKING TO GOD

God, sometimes people say things that make me wonder if I'm doing something wrong in my grief. From here forward, I'm going to grieve my own way, in my own time, upheld and guided by You.

DAY 3 — Where do you look for comfort?

"Junk food."
"I buy shoes."
"Spending time with my grandkids."
"I pray and read my Bible."
"I numb the pain any way I can."

Are the things that bring you comfort helping you, or hurting you?

GOD'S MESSAGE TO YOU

"My people ... have forsaken me, the spring of living water, and have dug their own cisterns, broken cisterns that cannot hold water." (Jeremiah 2:13)

1. What types of things do you find comforting? List as many things as you can think of.

"Pain is very personal." –Carla

2. What have you done in an attempt to relieve the pain that were not good choices (see today's Bible verse)?

3. To keep from prolonging your grief, you need to find relief in ways that take you closer to God. Write ideas of things you can do to move closer to God.

CONSIDER THIS

"The loss is still going to be there after you've eaten the half gallon of ice cream or drank a fifth or done something else, but you will have added a layer of problems that impairs your ability to face your first problem."
–Susan Lutz

TALKING TO GOD

God, I'm tired of hurting. Sometimes I'll do pretty much anything for a moment of relief. I need Your help with this. I can't do this on my own. Show me Your comfort.

DAY 4

How to find refuge
Emotional storms are slamming you. You long for a place of safety and refuge. But where? How?

GOD'S MESSAGE TO YOU
"Keep me safe, my God, for in you I take refuge." (Psalm 16:1)

"I know the LORD is always with me. I will not be shaken, for he is right beside me ... My body rests in safety." (Psalm 16:8–9 NLT)

1. Where does Psalm 16:1 say you will find refuge?

2. According to Psalm 16:8–9, where is God when you are at your shakiest, most vulnerable times?

3. Taking refuge in God involves turning to Him for protection and trusting that He will keep you safe no matter what comes. Why has this been hard for you? Or, how have you benefited from turning to and trusting Him?

CONSIDER THIS

Turn to God by:

- **Praying** – Pray a Psalm daily.
- **Listening to what He says** – Read the Care Cards in the back of this book.
- **Learning who He is** – Consider that you might have misconceptions about who He is. Spend time getting to know Him in the Bible.
- **Obeying Him** – God wants you to follow His directives. As you get more familiar with what the Bible says, look for ways to apply what you read.

TALKING TO GOD

God, in my storms and darkness, I long for a place of safety and security. This is only found in You. I run to You. Every time I try to turn back and live in unsafe places in my mind, help me run to You again.

"Don't marry somebody just because you're lonely." –Mike

Our responsibility

You can turn to God because of who He is. If you learn God's character, you'll be more likely to trust Him. But you are responsible to choose to do so.

GOD'S MESSAGE TO YOU

"The LORD is a refuge for the oppressed, a stronghold in times of trouble. Those who know your name trust in you, for you, LORD, have never forsaken those who seek you." (Psalm 9:9–10)

1. What does the Lord promise in Psalm 9:9–10?

2. Why do you think knowing more about God's name (His character) would help you trust Him in difficult times?

3. How has God been a refuge for you?

CONSIDER THIS

"God's comfort is to be sought." –Phil Sasser

"I realized I had a choice. I decided I was choosing God." –Cindy Bultema

*"I can trust Him because He has moved toward me and demonstrated His love and faithfulness."** –Susan Lutz

* See page xii to learn how and when God moved toward you and demonstrated His love and faithfulness.

TALKING TO GOD

God, the relationship I had with my loved one was one-of-a-kind. When I worry that I'm not grieving the right way, help me understand that I don't need to be anyone but the person You created me to be.

MIKE: LOOKING BACK

"I finally listened to God. The whole time He was trying to comfort me and I was not listening. I was not relying on what I'd read and heard and what I really believed [about Him]. I was letting my emotions take over my whole life. I had gone past the grieving and just was feeling sorry for myself.

"I can look back and see that God was right there the whole time. The times I was crying, He was comforting me. I'd lost my wife, and my life had changed, but I knew that God still had something for me, as He does for everybody. He does love us; He will not leave us."

NEXT SESSION
Learn practical tips to make it through the difficult days ahead.

"We all try to fix things, and I couldn't fix that." –Mike

MY WEEKLY GRIEF WORK

Session - Two

PERSONAL CHECKUP – TRACK YOUR HEALING PROGRESS
Place a check in the box identifying how you're feeling. Insert words to explain why.

	REALLY BAD	OKAY	PRETTY GOOD	GREAT
EMOTIONALLY				
PHYSICALLY				
SPIRITUALLY				
RELATIONALLY				

JOURNAL TOPICS – MAKING SENSE OF IT ALL
Choose one or more ideas below, or choose your own topic. We encourage
you to use a separate notebook for your weekly journaling.

✎ Describe what you miss most about your loved one.

✎ Describe how grief makes you feel like you're losing your mind.

✎ What things comfort you in your grief and how do these contrast with the way family members and friends find comfort?

MOVING FORWARD – PRACTICAL STEPS TOWARD HEALING
HOW TO START UNRAVELING YOUR TANGLED EMOTIONS
In order to sort through your mess of emotions, you must first identify,
or recognize, which emotions you're experiencing.

1. Turn to the "Common Responses to the Death of a Loved One" article on page 4.

2. Place a check next to those emotions you've experienced.

3. Add new ideas to the list of grief responses you've experienced.

4. Look at each response you did not mark and consider if it's an emotion you actually do have that you didn't realize. (For instance, many people do not think they are bitter about something, but later discover they are.)

Access your free resources

HELP & DIRECTION WHEN YOU NEED IT

GRIEFSHARE.ORG/MY

Free online help from GriefShare

View the GriefShare session videos
Watch again or catch up on those you missed.

 Activate your daily emails
Sign up for "A Season of Grief," 365 days of encouragement.

Discover bonus content
View bonus videos from your favorite experts and personal stories.

 Access classic videos
See the entire past edition of GriefShare.

 Get holiday help
Find tips to help you through the Thanksgiving and Christmas season.

More help is available!

GRIEFSHARE.ORG/MY

THE JOURNEY OF GRIEF - PART ONE

3
SESSION

SINCE THE DEATH OF YOUR LOVED ONE, you've started a journey. It's not a trip you planned, but it's a trip you must take. Several factors will shape your journey, and you can take intentional steps to point yourself in a healthy, healing direction. So, put on your hiking boots, get out your compass (Bible), and with the help of God and other people, you can avoid getting lost in the deep woods of grief.

After viewing the video, taking part in discussion, and completing your **FROM MOURNING TO JOY** exercises, you'll discover:

 Helpful goals to set on your journey of grief

How to deal with those who try to rush you through your grief

How long the journey of grief typically lasts

VIDEO OUTLINE

Use this outline to write down important concepts, encouraging words, or questions you have while viewing the video.

YOUR JOURNEY OF GRIEF

Does a new normal mean forgetting? (Psalm 23:4)

It's unique

Why it's unique

"Turning to Him is the best thing you can do." –Phil Sasser

Finding comfort

GOALS FOR YOUR JOURNEY

1. Acceptance

2. Turn to God   (Psalm 63:1)

3. Express your emotions

4. Establish a new identity

ADVICE FOR YOUR JOURNEY

Don't rush

People will try to rush you

"Never will I leave you; never will I forsake you." –God (Hebrews 13:5b)

Dealing with those who rush you

SURPRISES ON THE JOURNEY

You may feel relief or joy

Your pain may get worse

Ambushes of grief

SURVIVING YOUR JOURNEY

Don't numb your pain   (Isaiah 55:2)

Take your time

In this week's From Mourning to Joy exercises ...

Susan didn't have anyone she could honestly share her emotions with. She found this made her grief process last even longer. Find out how to work through some important goals of grief.

"The more you keep your emotions inside, the more they'll come out." –Dr. Robert DeVries

HOW TO WRITE A GRIEF LETTER

People mean well in their attempts to help you, but sometimes their efforts make things harder for you. It's helpful to write your friends and family what we call a "grief letter" so they can provide help that's best suited to you.

HOW TO WRITE A GRIEF LETTER:

1. Briefly describe your experience and your feelings.

2. Let people know what they can expect from you.

3. Tell them what they can do and say that you'd find comforting, and what's not comforting to you.

4. List specific, practical needs they can help with.

WHEN WRITING YOUR LETTER, REMEMBER:

- Share only your immediate needs. As your needs change, you can send or share a new letter.

- People won't be offended if you tell them exactly how to help you. They will appreciate your clear instructions. It takes the guesswork out of serving you.

- If you don't tell people what you need, you risk not being cared for and/or receiving unwanted help.

H. Norman Wright shares this sample grief letter in his book *Recovering from Losses in Life*.

Dear Friend (family, pastor, fellow workers ...),

Recently I have suffered a devastating loss. I am grieving and it will take months and even years to recover from this loss. I wanted to let you know that I will cry from time to time. I don't apologize for my tears since they are not a sign of weakness or a lack of faith. They are God's gift to me to express the extent of my loss, and they are also a sign that I am recovering.

At times you may see me angry for no apparent reason. Sometimes I'm not sure why. All I know is that my emotions are intense because of my grief. If I don't always make sense to you, please be forgiving and patient with me. And if I repeat myself again and again, please accept this as normal.

More than anything else I need your understanding and your presence. You don't always have to know what to say, or even say anything, if you don't know how to respond. Your presence and a touch or hug lets me know you care. Please don't wait for me to call you since sometimes I am too tired or tearful to do so. If I tend to withdraw from you, please don't let me do that. I need you to reach out to me for several months.

Pray for me that I would come to see meaning in my loss someday and that I would know God's comfort and love. It does help to let me know that you are praying for me. If you have experienced a similar type of loss, please feel free to share it with me ...

This loss is so painful, and right now it feels like the worst thing that could ever happen to me. But I will survive and eventually recover ...

Thank you for caring about me. Thank you for listening and praying. Your concern comforts me and is a gift for which I will always be thankful.

(Revell, 2006)

SUSAN: "I FELT LIKE I WAS ALONE"

"When I lost my mother, it was like becoming an orphan. She was my last close living relative. I felt like I was alone in the world. Being the only caregiver for Mother, my life had been wrapped up in taking care of her. When she had passed, a lot of that was immediately gone. I felt like I didn't have any purpose. I had no one to talk to, to get out some of my feelings. My friends didn't want to hear about it anymore, so I would throw a mask up to try to act like everything was okay."

If you hesitate to be honest about your emotional state, if other people are rushing you through grief, or if you have fears about your future, you'll find it helpful to work through the ideas and strategies in this week's study.

DAY 1

Express your emotions
Expressing your emotions can be scary. But God will comfort you when you do. *"It's good to talk it out. You will get through to the other side."* –Susan

GOD'S MESSAGE TO YOU
"He has sent me [Jesus] ... to comfort all who mourn." (Isaiah 61:1b–2)

1. Are you allowing yourself to express your grief? Why or why not?

2. According to Isaiah 61:1b–2, what is one reason God sent Jesus?

3. Why do you think God wants you to know that Jesus is more than a great moral teacher, savior, or miracle worker–but that He is also a comforter?

4. We've suggested a few ways you can experience Jesus's comfort. Add your ideas to the list.

    a. Reading the Bible.

    b. Listening to others share how God has helped them heal.

    c. _____

    d. _____

"I wore a mask to try to hide my feelings." –Susan

TALKING TO GOD

God, I know I have to release these emotions in order to heal. Help me to grieve honestly over the suffering and sorrow in my life and in this world, and then to seek, anticipate, and accept the comfort You have for me.

 DAY 2

Accept the reality of your loved one's death

A goal of grieving you learned on this week's video is to face the reality that you are here and your loved one is not coming back.

GOD'S MESSAGE TO YOU

"The LORD said to Joshua ... 'Moses my servant is dead. Now then, you and all these people, get ready ... because you will lead these people to inherit the land I swore to their ancestors to give them.'" (Joshua 1:1b–2, 6)

1. As Moses's successor, Joshua inherited the huge responsibility of leading the Israelite nation. Before God instructed Joshua on what to do, what did He remind him of (see today's Bible verses)?

2. Why do you think it was important for Joshua to accept the reality that Moses was dead in order for him to move forward with what God had for him?

3. Why is it important (and painful) for you to accept the reality that your loved one is dead?

CONSIDER THIS

"I had to tell myself that I lost my father and he was gone, and that was the first real step towards grieving for me." –Amy

SEASONS CHANGE

"When you make your way through grief, you don't leave that person behind. You bring that person with you, where your memories of that person and your thankfulness for that person [become] a happy experience and not filled with so much pain." –Susan Lutz

TALKING TO GOD

God, my loved one is no longer here. I don't like it and I don't want it, but I recognize that it's true. Help me to do the tough work of grief in order to make it through.

 DAY 3

Develop a new identity

"Who am I without my loved one?" Now that your loved one is gone, you will have to figure out who you are now. But there are some things that will never change.

"I came to realize I had never really grieved my dad." –Susan

GOD'S MESSAGE TO YOU

"See what great love the Father has lavished on us, that we should be called children of God! And that is what we are!" (1 John 3:1a)

"My sheep listen to my voice; I know them, and they follow me. I give them eternal life, and they shall never perish; no one will snatch them out of my hand." (John 10:27–28)

1. If you are a Christian, according to 1 John 3:1a what are you also?

2. In John 10:27–28, Jesus calls His followers His sheep. What does Jesus give His sheep?

3. When Jesus says no one will snatch His sheep/ followers out of His hand, He means their relationship with Him is secure. If you're a Christian, how does it encourage you to know your relationship with God is stable, secure, never at risk (despite the changes you're dealing with)?

CONSIDER THIS

"Who am I? What really defines my existence? I want that to be based on something that can never be lost."
–Dr. Stephen Viars

TALKING TO GOD

God, it's time for me to figure out who I really am, to gain some solid footing in my shifting world. I want to know what it truly means to be loved by You, to be Your child, to have eternal life, and how I can live in that constant security no matter what comes my way.

 DAY 4 | **I have so many fears**
Fears about the future, fears about today, fears for family members, fears about creating a new normal and moving forward ...

GOD'S MESSAGE TO YOU

"God is our refuge and strength, an ever-present help in trouble. Therefore we will not fear, though the earth give way and the mountains fall into the heart of the sea, though its waters roar and foam and the mountains quake with their surging." (Psalm 46:1–3)

1. What can you relate to in Psalm 46:1–3?

2. When your earth has given way beneath you, and the waters are roaring around you, where is God (according to Psalm 46:1–3)?

3. Turning to God for help is an intentional act in times of anxiety. How can you make turning to God a habit when fears come?

"Just hang on to His love." –Susan

"When I'm in a place of anxiety, I stop and say, 'What am I dwelling on?' and it's all the areas where I'm just not able." –Sandy Elder

TALKING TO GOD

God, I'm struggling with unbelief and fear. Help me to hold tightly to Your ever-present hand. Your presence helps relieve my fears. Keep me safe and strong.

DAY 5 — When people try to rush you

Don't let people rush you past the pain. They are not the authority on your grief.

GOD'S MESSAGE TO YOU

"There is a time for everything, and a season for every activity under the heavens: a time to be born and a time to die, a time to plant and a time to uproot ... a time to tear down and a time to build, a time to weep and a time to laugh, a time to mourn and a time to dance." (Ecclesiastes 3:1–4)

1. Describe when you've felt rushed or pressured by someone to get through your grief.

2. Based upon Ecclesiastes 3:1–4, what does God think you should be doing during this season of your life?

3. How might these verses from Ecclesiastes help you respond to someone who asks why you are so sad right now and whether or not your happiness will return?

"We don't get through grieving at least until the first anniversary of [the] death. And that's really fast. Most people, it takes two to three to sometimes even four years to really go through that grief journey." –Dr. Susan Zonnebelt-Smeenge

TALKING TO GOD

God, hold me firmly in Your everlasting arms as I try to face the tough work of grief.

SUSAN: LOOKING BACK

"After Mother passed away, I was fearful about what my future would be. Thankfully, I have come to realize I have people that would be there for me if I needed them, and God has always provided for me; for instance, shortly after Mother passed away, God gave me a job right when I needed it.

"Through everything I've been through, Mother's [death], my dad, loss of job, loss of friends, God has always been there, and He always will be there for me. And I tell myself, 'Susan, it's going to be okay; just walk through it, take hold of the people that are willing to help you, and you will get through this with God's love.'"

NEXT SESSION
Discover things you can do to make your grief journey more bearable.

Time is not the healer of wounds. God is.

MY WEEKLY GRIEF WORK

Session - Three

PERSONAL CHECKUP – TRACK YOUR HEALING PROGRESS

Place a check in the box identifying how you're feeling. Insert words to explain why.

	REALLY BAD	OKAY	PRETTY GOOD	GREAT
EMOTIONALLY				
PHYSICALLY				
SPIRITUALLY				
RELATIONALLY				

JOURNAL TOPICS – MAKING SENSE OF IT ALL

Choose one or more ideas below, or choose your own topic. We encourage you to use a separate notebook for your weekly journaling.

 Write down things you always want to remember about your loved one.

 Write down good lessons you've learned from your loved one and character traits you want to emulate and pass on to others.

 Describe a special memory.

MOVING FORWARD – PRACTICAL STEPS TOWARD HEALING
HOW TO STORE MEMORIES OF YOUR LOVED ONE

One of the goals of grief is to store memories of your loved one. In the space below, brainstorm numerous ideas of ways you can store memories of your loved one. Here are some ideas.

○ Send a letter to several people asking them to write down a treasured memory and send it back to you. Have these bound in a book.

○ Plan a get-together with family/friends to share stories of your loved one.

○ Visit places you and your loved one used to go.

○ Make a scrapbook or picture collage.

○ Incorporate and pass on character traits you learned from your loved one.

○ Do volunteer work or create a tribute in honor of a cause that your loved one had a heart for.

THE JOURNEY OF GRIEF - PART TWO

THE GRIEF JOURNEY SEEMS TOO LONG. Too hard. Too painful. You avoid places that remind you of your loved one, with no thought of ever going there again. You've no desire to change a single item in your loved one's bedroom. Some days all you consume are coffee and chips, because cooking takes up too much energy.

These factors all play a part in determining the length of your grief journey. Through this week's video, discussion, and workbook exercises, you'll become more aware of:

 Why it's important to put effort into your healing

Λ How the events surrounding your loved one's death affect your grief

Λ The best ways to deal with your loved one's belongings

VIDEO OUTLINE

Use this outline to write down important concepts, encouraging words, or questions you have while viewing the video.

FACTORS AFFECTING YOUR GRIEF

Self-care

How & when a loved one died

Life events

"Going to those places that hurt too much is the very thing that heals us." –Gail

Your efforts to heal   (Isaiah 42:3)

Your loved one's belongings

Your Loved One's Belongings

They help you heal

Sort them yourself

Turning to God   (James 4:8)

Journaling

"Ask others for help." –Joyce Rogers

In this week's From Mourning to Joy exercises ...

You'll hear how David was hesitant to ask for help after his wife died, but found it was necessary. He also shares practical tips on how he's relied on God to meet his needs. You'll find helpful suggestions for your grief journey this week.

How to watch session videos online

Log on to **griefshare.org/my** to watch full GriefShare session videos. It's a great option if you:

- Missed a meeting and want to see the video
- Want to rewatch something you saw
- Want to review before your group meeting

Watch the videos today!

GRIEFSHARE.ORG/MY

"God's comfort is to be sought." –Phil Sasser

HOW TO ASK FOR AND ACCEPT HELP

"God is the source and supply of what you need," says Dr. Paul David Tripp, "but God uses instruments, and God's got a lot of tools in His toolbox. You were created for community; you weren't wired to do this by yourself. It's a great question to ask: Who are those good instruments that God has put in my life? How can I take advantage of those relationships?"

If you want to experience healing from the pain, wholeness, and peace, then you need the Lord and you need to allow Him to use other people to help. People want to help you and are able to help you, if you will allow them and offer some direction.

MOST PEOPLE DON'T KNOW WHAT YOU NEED

Many times people have no idea of what would truly be helpful to you. They may bring food, when what you really need is a babysitter or a mechanic. They may think you're doing fine and don't need help–when actually you do. It is important to be assertive in this situation. People want to help, so do not deny them this opportunity, which can be a blessing for both of you!

HOW CAN OTHERS HELP? WHAT CAN YOU ASK OF OTHERS?

If you need a hand with the housework or yard, need a healthy role-model for your children, are struggling to create a budget, are juggling too many tasks at work, or need someone to listen and not offer advice–let your needs be known. Perhaps you need help with holiday planning, meal preparation, decorating, or taking your children shopping or to special events.

"Let your friends, relatives, and coworkers know you will need help and what type of help you'll need. In a moment of crisis, it's difficult to say exactly what it is you need, but whatever it is that you might need, go ahead and call now," advises Sabrina D. Black.

BE HONEST

Jennifer shares from her experiences, "Be honest with friends and family and ask them to pray for you. I know their prayers held me up so many times." Let people know what they can pray for specifically, and not just that you will "make it through." Ask them to pray that you will draw closer to the Lord and find deep, inner peace; that you'll be able to extend help and support to others; and that you'll experience a strength that you've never before had. Ask them to pray that you'll have the constant assurance you're not alone.

Asking for and accepting help is an important part of living in a community and being in relationship with others. Ask God whom to approach for help, and reach out and let someone help you. You will be glad you did!

DAVID: "EVERYTHING FELL ON ME"

"Carol and I were doing pretty good [financially] because her social security covered the house payment and with mine it was bills, groceries, gas, and maybe going out to eat a couple times. When she passed away, everything fell on me, and I got put into a financial hardship.

"I'm a hard person to take help from somebody. I'm one of these people who feels like he's always bothering somebody else, but I'm trying to learn and everybody keeps telling me, 'Don't feel that way. Ask for the help and let's go on.'"

Perhaps you don't like to ask others for help, preferring instead to handle things on your own. Setting aside pride and asking for needed help is part of your healing process. We need other people in our lives, and we need God.

 DAY 1 **Your efforts to heal**
Grief lasts longer than you might have expected, but putting forth effort to do your grief work will help you heal.

GOD'S MESSAGE TO YOU
"How long, LORD? ... How long must I wrestle with my thoughts and day after day have sorrow in my heart? ... But I trust in your unfailing love, my heart rejoices in your salvation. I will sing the LORD's praise, for he has been good to me." (Psalm 13:1–2, 5–6)

1. What thoughts do you have about how long your grief and pain is lasting?

2. What three things did the author of today's Psalm do to encourage himself in the midst of his sorrow?

   a.

   b.

   c.

3. What steps can you take, or what goals of grief are you willing to work on, that would move you toward healing?

"I'm a big believer that the Lord will take care of me." –David

CONSIDER THIS

Reflecting on God's love doesn't instantly remove your sorrow, but it can ease your pain and give you hope.

"The stable things in your life are going to help you through the ups and downs of grief: going to God, going to God's Word, fellowship with other Christians."
–Phil Sasser

TALKING TO GOD

God, the Bible says You are stable and unchanging. Your love for me doesn't ebb and flow; it's constant and strong. I want to keep trusting in Your steadfast love in the midst of my unpredictable life.

BE SURE TO COMPLETE THE MY WEEKLY GRIEF WORK SECTION EACH WEEK.

DAY 2

Look expectantly for healing
We have to wait for healing. We can't force it to happen. But we can learn to wait expectantly.

GOD'S MESSAGE TO YOU
"I wait for the LORD, my whole being waits, and in his word I put my hope." (Psalm 130:5)

1. In Psalm 130:5, how engaged is the psalmist in the waiting process?

2. What does the psalmist do while he waits?

3. The word for "hope" in the Bible does not refer to wishful thinking or "I hope so." This hope means an absolute certainty that something will come to pass. You can put your hope in God's Word by reading it, obeying it, and trusting in it. What changes will you make in your daily life to start putting your hope in God's Word?

4. Write down a Bible verse (you can choose one from your workbook, if desired) that you will put your hope in.

CONSIDER THIS

"God has called me to grow in some areas where before there was no growth. I need to be intentional to press into the Lord and to do those things well that He's called me to do." –Carla

TALKING TO GOD

God, I wait expectantly for the relief and comfort that will come from You. I'm not sure what it will look like, or when it will come, but I want to be in the right position to receive it.

DAY 3

You need help from others
We were created to help one another in love. That includes being a willing recipient. Define your needs, and ask for specific help from others.

GOD'S MESSAGE TO YOU
Exodus 17 tells of a battle that was raging between two nations. Moses was standing on a hill above the battle, holding up the staff of God. As long as his hands were held up, his people were winning. But when he lowered them, the other nation gained the advantage.

"It's good to have help. I can't do it by myself." –Shay

"But Moses' hands grew weary, so ... Aaron and Hur held up his hands, one on one side, and the other on the other side. So his hands were steady until the going down of the sun." (Exodus 17:12 ESV)

1. What does Moses allow his friends to do in Exodus 17:12?

2. What was the result (see Exodus 17:12)?

3. Why do you hesitate to ask people for help?

CONSIDER THIS

"At first I was very shy to ask for help. I'd think, 'I should be able to do this.'" –Marne

"If I believe I'm self-sufficient, grieving situations will prove I was wrong about that." –Dr. Stephen Viars

TALKING TO GOD

God, I don't want to bother people; they have their own things going on. But despite these thoughts, I know I can't do this on my own. Give me the grace to ask for specific help and to accept it.

 DAY 4

When pride holds you back

Have you considered that not asking for help can be a form of pride? Asking for help requires humility, and it shows a willingness to depend on God for your needs. Many times God provides for our needs through other people.

GOD'S MESSAGE TO YOU

"Do you see a person wise in their own eyes? There is more hope for a fool than for them." (Proverbs 26:12)

"When pride comes, then comes disgrace, but with humility comes wisdom." (Proverbs 11:2)

1. What areas of your life do you try to handle on your own, when you know deep down a little help would be beneficial?

2. Proverbs 26:12 mentions a person who is wise in his own eyes. Everyone can relate to that at some level. What does the proverb say about such a person?

3. How does Proverbs 11:2 challenge the thinking of the person who believes that asking for help is disgraceful? According to this passage, what is actually disgraceful?

"To admit I needed help was a whole new adventure for me." –Cindy Bultema

CONSIDER THIS

"I was raised very independent, very private. 'You don't need help, just figure it out. Life is hard. Keep moving.' But when David was killed, I realized, 'I can't do this on my own. This is too big.' As difficult as it was to receive the help, I would have been foolish not to." –Cindy Bultema

TALKING TO GOD

God, show me the areas in my life where I need to let go of my pride and humbly depend on You and others.

DAY 5 — God can guide you out of the darkness

Your willingness to turn to God shapes your journey of healing.

GOD'S MESSAGE TO YOU

"Where can I go from your Spirit? Where can I flee from your presence? If I go up to the heavens, you are there; if I make my bed in the depths, you are there." (Psalm 139:7–8)

"Look to the LORD and his strength; seek his face always." (1 Chronicles 16:11)

"Anyone who comes to him must believe that he exists and that he rewards those who earnestly seek him." (Hebrews 11:6b)

1. If you feel that God has abandoned you, where has He been, according to Psalm 139:7–8?

2. Even though God is everywhere, what does 1 Chronicles 16:11 tell us to do?

3. According to Hebrews 11:6b, what are two requirements of all those who go to (or seek) God?

CONSIDER THIS

"God is sustaining us, strengthening us, even when we're unaware of that. God's comfort is to be sought as well. In some sense, [the experience of comfort is] not automatic. There is a component to it that God says, 'Draw near unto God, and He will draw near unto you.'" –Phil Sasser

HOW OTHERS HAVE TURNED TO GOD

"Admitting my weaknesses and that I need help." –Donna

"I kept reading my Bible." –Carla

"I pray a lot." –Barbara

"Every day seek the Lord, hear Him, and be filled with the Holy Spirit so I can do what I need to do." –Carla

"Praising the Lord and thanking Him." –Sandy

TALKING TO GOD

One way I can choose to turn to You is through prayer. Help me to find more ways to turn to You throughout my days and throughout my nights. You are always there for me.

"The real answer is the presence of God." –Michael Card

DAVID: LOOKING BACK

"From the pride perspective, you don't want to admit things are rough, but in this situation you wake up real quick. You have to face your reality that life has to go on and you have to deal with what you are given. You can either throw your hands up and run away, or you can put it in God's hands and let Him fill your needs as you go along.

"Now we have to be patient, and patience is a big thing, especially when you are letting the Lord lead you and take care of you. You have to let Him do His will for your life, and it may not be the way you think it should be done, but we know His will is perfect and it's exactly meant for us. That's the way I live day-to-day and just let the Lord meet my needs. He's not let me down yet, and I don't think He ever will."

NEXT SESSION
See how grief affects your relationships and what you can do about it.

MY WEEKLY GRIEF WORK

Session - Four

PERSONAL CHECKUP – TRACK YOUR HEALING PROGRESS

Place a check in the box identifying how you're feeling. Insert words to explain why.

	REALLY BAD	OKAY	PRETTY GOOD	GREAT
EMOTIONALLY				
PHYSICALLY				
SPIRITUALLY				
RELATIONALLY				

JOURNAL TOPICS – MAKING SENSE OF IT ALL

Choose one or more ideas below, or choose your own topic. We encourage you to use a separate notebook for your weekly journaling.

- Write down what you've done or plan to do with your loved one's belongings. What fears or worries do you have about this?

- Describe some favorite places you used to go to with your loved one. Talk to God about the possibility of going to one of those places again without your loved one, as part of your grief work.

MOVING FORWARD – PRACTICAL STEPS TOWARD HEALING
HOW TO BE PREPARED TO RECEIVE HELP

When people ask, "How can I help?" it's important to be prepared with answers. On a separate paper, (1) write down different areas where help is needed, (2) make a list of ways people could help, and (3) give your list to people willing to help. Here are ideas to get you started.

Areas I could use help:

Household chores, indoor/outdoor
- Someone to do a specific chore
- Instructions on how to do a chore
- Recommendations of someone to hire
- Someone to watch the kids so I can do a chore

Finances/Job
- Help with a financial need
- Wise counsel on financial decisions

- Guidance on how to budget
- Help with a job search

Companionship/Friendships
- Someone to listen and not offer advice
- Phone calls
- Friendly cards
- Someone who will pray with me

Free online help from GriefShare

BONUS VIDEOS, ARTICLES, TIPS &
DAILY EMAILS JUST FOR YOU

Access your <u>free</u> GriefShare resources today!

GRIEFSHARE.ORG/MY

FREE DAILY EMAIL ENCOURAGEMENT

SIGN UP FOR "A SEASON OF GRIEF."
RECEIVE AN UPLIFTING EMAIL MESSAGE EACH DAY FOR A YEAR.

"I look for the wonderful, inspirational messages I get from you in the morning.
Your thoughts are much better than what runs through my head during this time."

"They helped me through despair, anxiety, many tearful days."

GRIEFSHARE.ORG/MY

GRIEF SHARE

YOU MIGHT HAVE BEEN SURPRISED to find that some of your relationships have changed after your loved one's death. People you thought would remain close have drifted away; people you didn't know well before have come closer. Dealing with relationships can be confusing during grief. But relationships are crucial to your healing.

As you view the video and complete your **FROM MOURNING TO JOY** and **MY WEEKLY GRIEF WORK** exercises, you'll have a more focused understanding of:

- How the death of a loved one affects your friendships

- Why solitude can be a blessing and a curse

- How to deal with friends who don't understand your grief

VIDEO OUTLINE

Use this outline to write down important concepts, encouraging words, or questions you have while viewing the video.

GRIEF & RELATIONSHIPS

Family members grieve uniquely

Intense loneliness

No one understands

"Communication needs to be, first of all, loving." –Carla

Don't isolate

Benefits of solitude

No excuse to be rude

Jealousy

Friendships change

Why friendships change

STAY CONNECTED TO OTHERS

Create boundaries

Make new friends

"Sometimes we have high expectations of how people are going to be." –Sheila

Expect offense

Be merciful   (Ephesians 4:32)

Dealing with "truth"

In this week's From Mourning to Joy exercises ...

Barbara struggles with feelings of loneliness, even while surrounded by other people. You'll find suggestions on ways to deal with loneliness and how time alone and time with others can help you.

"The truth is that God can equip other people to care for us." –Carla

CARING FOR GRIEVING CHILDREN

Perhaps you feel you can barely keep your own life together, much less take care of someone else. But your children need you. Yes, it is difficult to care for your children when you're grieving, but these suggestions will help.

Be authentic – Your kids are watching you for direction on how to handle their own grief. Model for them that it's okay to cry, be sad, and talk about your loved one. Also model, with authenticity, how to walk through grief: that means doing your grief work, and most importantly, turning to God.

Children grieve intermittently – Unlike adults, children will experience strong emotions, but then take a break. The next thing you know, they're playing, laughing, and having fun. Recognize that your child is grieving and be there to help, but also allow your child to be a child.

Your children may not grieve the same way you do – Just because your children do not express grief as much or in the same way as you does not mean they aren't grieving deeply. "Provide opportunities for them to express themselves. Acknowledge whatever it is that they're feeling. When they're asking you to leave them alone, respect that; and when they're asking you to be close, try to be there for them," advises David Bueno Martin.

Give truthful, age-appropriate responses to your children's questions – "You need to give as much information as the children can handle according to their age level, and you've got to be honest," says H. Norman Wright.

Be on the lookout for abnormal behavior – It's normal for school grades to suffer, eating habits to change, and for a child to be sad. But if your child begins behaving erratically–particularly in a way that's counter to his or her personality–consider seeking the help of someone experienced in helping children in grief. If your child begins talking about committing suicide, immediately seek the help of a professional who is trained in helping suicidal people.

Get help – Your child is your responsibility, but it's helpful to ask a relative, family friend, or youth/children's pastor to spend time with your child and help the child deal with his or her grief. This will give your child someone else to talk to about his or her feelings. It will also give you the opportunity to get some rest and deal with personal issues; then you'll be better able to focus on your child when you are back together again.

Clarify family roles – If a member of the immediate family dies, make sure everyone knows his or her expected roles in the family now. For instance, don't put an unnecessary burden on a male child to be the "man of the house" and somehow take on the role of the deceased dad. Allow the child to be a child, and be clear about that.

The online video "**How to Help Grieving Children**" offers many more suggestions on how to care for your grieving children. View this video at *www.griefshare.org/children*.

BEING HONEST WITH YOUR COMFORTERS

In an attempt to comfort you, many times people will say or do things that have the opposite effect. Most people are well-meaning, but they do not know how to react to you or how to best help you.

The solution to this dilemma is for you to be honest about your feelings with people and to communicate your needs and concerns—this can be done in person or in a letter. Often, the best time to communicate is before you end up in an uncomfortable situation with a well-meaning, but clueless, comforter.

THEY WON'T KNOW UNLESS YOU TELL THEM

"If somebody is trying to walk alongside of you after a significant loss," says Dr. Robert DeVries, "this person has no clue about how you feel, what you think, what you need, and what you want. The only solution is to tell them."

H. Norman Wright says that for those people who are trying to rush you through grief, it is best to say, "I appreciate what you're trying to do, but my grief is going to last probably twenty times longer than most people expect. It's going to be more intense. Let me cry; let me feel the way I'm feeling. I would deeply appreciate it. To help you understand me, here's a little book on grief, and by reading this, you'll have a better idea of what's going on within me."*

"It's so important to be honest with people," explains Elsa Kok Colopy, Christian speaker and author. "Many times we feel like we need to cover up our bad feelings, cover up our sadness, cover up our grief for the benefit of others. You don't have to do that. You can express what you need."

* One suggestion of a book to give to others is *Grieving with Hope* by Samuel J. Hodges IV and Kathy Leonard.

WRITE A GRIEF LETTER

H. Norman Wright suggests that you write a grief letter (see page 24) to pass out to your comforters, which will help them know how to best relate to you during this time. "In that letter you identify here's what I've experienced, here's what's going on with me, and here's what you can expect from me. You don't have to try to fix me. Let me cry, and I'll recover in my own timing. Here are the best things for you to do." You then identify what you need from people in the letter, and pass this out or send it in an email. When people ask, "How are you?" simply respond, "Thanks for asking, here ... this will explain it better than I can." This is a positive action you can take to help your comforters, and ultimately, to help you!

Take a moment to think about situations you've experienced where your would-be comforters were insensitive in their attempts to help you. Now, in response to those situations, what do you wish your comforters would have done differently? What do you wish they understood about your grief? What helpful advice could you give to your comforters?

WHAT YOU MIGHT SHARE WITH YOUR COMFORTERS

Here are ideas of needs or concerns you might want to communicate to people around you:

- Please talk about my deceased loved one.

- Be a quiet listener, and let me talk about my loved one and share memories.

- Ignoring my grief does not make it go away.

- If I am sad, let me be sad. Do not try to cheer me up. It's important for me to feel the emotions I am feeling.

- Sometimes it may appear that I'm functioning fine and that I'm doing well. Understand that outward appearances can be deceiving.

- Don't make comments about next year being better or time healing my wounds; my concerns are focused on the here and now.

- Understand that I can't do everything I used to do in the past, but don't hesitate to invite me to do things anyway.

- Let me cry if I need to. You don't have to say anything—just hand me tissues and be there for me.

- Understand that grief can go on for a number of years. There is no established time limit.

- Please don't make judgments about how long it's taking me to grieve.

- Other ideas:

_____

The advice in this article, and any further ideas that you have, would be wonderful for your friends and family members to know. It would make things a bit easier not only for you, but also for your comforters. Make a point to practice being honest with people around you and to be assertive in communicating your needs.

BARBARA: "I COULDN'T GO BACK"

"I live in a small community. We've lived there since the seventies; the kids grew up there. My husband was very friendly, and when he passed, everybody knew it. I walked in the cleaners right after he died, and they all started crying, and it threw me totally. I couldn't go back there again.

"It's wonderful living in a community where everybody knows you, but it's very hard. Even though I have people around me, it's not the same thing. I still think about how alone I am."

Feelings of loneliness can occur whether you're by yourself or surrounded by other people. In this week's **From Mourning to Joy**, you'll find suggestions on how to deal with loneliness and the value of both time spent alone and time spent with other people.

DAY 1 — God is close to you

Have you ever stood in the middle of a group of people and felt utterly alone?

GOD'S MESSAGE TO YOU

"The LORD is close to the brokenhearted and saves those who are crushed in spirit." (Psalm 34:18)

1. At what moments have you felt farthest away from God? Why do you think this is?

2. During your journey of grief, when have you felt closest to God?

3. What does Psalm 34:18 indicate you should expect of God as you deal with your broken heart and crushed spirit?

CONSIDER THIS

"God comes closer at these times because He knows we are so compromised in our ability to even affirm the things we know." –Susan Lutz

Plan a weekend or a day, or just thirty minutes, to go someplace where you can be alone with God, perhaps to the lake, beach, mountains, or a local park. Talk with God about what's going on. Let Him ache with you, cry with you, and comfort you.

"It's good to share with someone who's experienced similar things." –Barbara

TALKING TO GOD

God, my spirit is crushed, and my heart is broken. Sometimes I can't feel You, but I know You are here. I will cling to that truth and be comforted by it.

 DAY 2 ### Dealing with loneliness
To help us deal with loneliness, God gives us Himself (His presence) and He puts us in community with other people.

GOD'S MESSAGE TO YOU
"Two are better than one, because they have a good return for their labor: If either of them falls down, one can help the other up. But pity anyone who falls and has no one to help them up." (Ecclesiastes 4:9–10)

1. What is the benefit of spending time with supportive, caring people, according to Ecclesiastes 4:9–10?

2. According to Ecclesiastes 4:9–10, what is the consequence of isolating yourself from other people?

3. What should you be doing to demonstrate that you believe the truths of Ecclesiastes 4:9–10?

CONSIDER THIS

"We are made for community."
–Ruth Graham

"There will be lonely nights and lonely moments, but realize God is always there. [He is] Emmanuel, which means 'God with us.'" –Sabrina D. Black

TALKING TO GOD

God, shutting myself off from other people will only prolong my grieving and make my loneliness worse. Help me to step out and rebuild old friendships and make new friends, too.

DAY 3 ### The benefits of being alone
Solitude, when used to spend intentional time alone with God, is important.

GOD'S MESSAGE TO YOU
"You will fill me with joy in your [God's] presence, with eternal pleasures at your right hand." (Psalm 16:11b)

1. We need to spend time with God in order to heal. According to Psalm 16:11b, what are some benefits of spending time in His presence?

2. What is the difference between isolating yourself from others and spending productive time alone with God?

3. In light of today's exercise, going forward, how will your time alone look different now?

"There are times that being alone with God is the only way to unburden your soul." –Julie Ganschow

"Bonhoeffer, the great martyr in Germany, said, 'If you desire community, seek solitude. If you desire solitude, seek community.' Both are crucial."
–Dr. Larry Crabb

TALKING TO GOD

God, I want to use my time alone to help myself heal. Please remind me to pray and to think helpful thoughts when I'm alone. And guide me to Scriptures and books to read and reflect upon.

People say hurtful things

DAY 4

Sometimes your friends can say some insensitive things. How does God want you to respond? His answers might surprise you.

GOD'S MESSAGE TO YOU

"Be merciful, just as your Father is merciful." (Luke 6:36)

"Pray for those who hurt you." (Luke 6:28b NLT)

"Those who are kind benefit themselves, but the cruel bring ruin on themselves." (Proverbs 11:17)

1. When someone said something hurtful to you, how did you respond?

2. What does the Bible say is the best way to respond (see Luke 6:28b, 36)?

3. According to Proverbs 11:17, when you respond to someone who has said something hurtful, who is most affected by your response?

CONSIDER THIS

"Nobody gets it right all the time, and someday I'll be the one who will say or do something a little odd, unhelpful, and I'm going to need their forgiveness."
–Carla

TALKING TO GOD

God, most of the people who comfort me have no idea what I am going through. Give me the strength to be patient with them and not put too high of expectations on them. Since You are the source of comfort, please guide me to people who can help me.

The desire for physical touch

DAY 5

"I miss just sitting there holding hands."
–Barbara

It's important to set boundaries and to find healthy, God-pleasing ways to help satisfy your desire for physical affection.

GOD'S MESSAGE TO YOU

"Flee from sexual immorality. All other sins a person commits are outside the body, but whoever sins sexually, sins against their own body ... Therefore honor God with your bodies." (1 Corinthians 6:18, 20b)

1. According to this passage, what should you do if you find yourself tempted (by your own thoughts or by the actions of another) to do something sexually immoral—whether you're sharing your grief with a person of the opposite sex, watching television, surfing the net, out on a date, or any other situation outside of a marital relationship?

"My feelings [about dating] started changing because of loneliness." –Stephen

2. Write down specific boundaries you will set for yourself to help you resist sexual temptation.

CONSIDER THIS

"Make sure you're through your grief before you even start dating anybody, because you're just asking for trouble." –Mike

"One of the reasons I'm intentional to keep my conversation with any man brief is that I want to be wise to protect certainly his relationship [with his wife] but also to protect my own heart from wanting a false security. The lie is that I can have what I imagine. The truth is that God is sovereign and He decides what we have and what we don't have." –Carla

TALKING TO GOD

God, I miss that physical touch and reassurance so much. Please help me to find ways to satisfy my need for a touch that please You.

BARBARA: LOOKING BACK

"One day I was sitting in my office and one of the associate pastors came in and sat down and said, 'I haven't talked to you in a while. How are you doing?' It gave me a feeling that I could actually talk to him about it, and I didn't realize I needed that. I felt he actually was caring, and I was able to share. I thanked him for doing that.

"I have known people who have lost someone, and I [used to] say, 'How are you doing?' But I'm saying it and walking at the same time, so people get the message that you're there, but you're not there. I'm seeing that more now since I've had a loss, that I did the same thing to other people. Sometimes all you need is someone you believe really cares about you and what's going on in your life."

NEXT SESSION
Bring your toughest questions and emotions to God. He can handle it.

MY WEEKLY GRIEF WORK

Session - Five

PERSONAL CHECKUP – TRACK YOUR HEALING PROGRESS

Place a check in the box identifying how you're feeling. Insert words to explain why.

	REALLY BAD	OKAY	PRETTY GOOD	GREAT
EMOTIONALLY				
PHYSICALLY				
SPIRITUALLY				
RELATIONALLY				

JOURNAL TOPICS – MAKING SENSE OF IT ALL

Choose one or more ideas below, or choose your own topic. We encourage you to use a separate notebook for your weekly journaling.

✎ Write a grief letter to your friends and family (see instructions on page 24).

✎ Where is God in your loneliness? Write a letter to God telling Him about your struggles with loneliness.

MOVING FORWARD – PRACTICAL STEPS TOWARD HEALING
SIGNS YOU'RE EXPECTING TOO MUCH FROM YOUR COMFORTERS

Expecting other people to know what you need, what you want, or what to say to you, without any direction from you, can harm relationships. Check any statements below that have been true for you.

○ I expect my comforters to know what to say without any guidance from me.

○ I expect them to know what I need without me telling them.

○ I expect them to place me as the center of attention when I want them to.

○ I expect them to understand the way I grieve.

○ I expect them to fill voids in my life that only God can fill.

○ I expect them to remain silent if I engage in harmful behaviors to numb my pain.

COMMUNICATE WITH YOUR COMFORTERS

Show your care for others by making it easier for them to care for you …

Let them know what you want them to say, and what not to say.

Give them a list of your specific needs (see last week's My Weekly Grief Work, page 41).

Give them a grief letter (see page 24).

Have mercy on them and forgive them, just as God has extended mercy and forgiveness to you.

WHY?

"WHY, GOD? WHY? IT'S SO UNFAIR. Please hear my cry and answer me!"
You likely have many questions surrounding your loved one's death. God wants you
to bring those questions to Him.

As you view the video and complete your **FROM MOURNING TO JOY** and
MY WEEKLY GRIEF WORK exercises, you'll have a more focused understanding of:

 God wants you to share your feelings with Him

 Why being honest with God is an expression of faith

 What God has to say to you about your "why" questions

VIDEO OUTLINE

Use this outline to write down important concepts, encouraging words, or questions
you have while viewing the video.

BE HONEST WITH GOD

Lament   (Job 3:20-21, 3:25-26, Psalm 22:1, 56:8)

It's an expression of faith

"A lament is a cry to Someone who is there." –Phil Sasser

WRONG ASSUMPTIONS

Intensify our pain

Intensify Our Pain

"Good people don't suffer"

"My plan is God's plan"

GOD'S RESPONSE TO JOB

"Do you know who I am?"   (Job 42:3b, 5)

"I STILL WANT ANSWERS!"

Must God respond?   (Job 38:4, Deuteronomy 29:29)

Are explanations helpful?   (Job 38–41)

"I can put my focus on the answers God has already given me." –Dr. Stephen Viars

GOD'S CHARACTER

A source of strength

A Source of Strength

God is sovereign   (Job 13:15a)

God is good   (1 John 4:10, John 3:16)

God understands   (Psalm 147:5, John 11:35)

TRUSTING WITHOUT ANSWERS

Dave & Sue's story   (Psalm 139:16)

In this week's From Mourning to Joy exercises ...

When God didn't answer her prayer to heal her son, Vaneetha questioned God and had to choose whether or not she was going to trust Him. Find out how to put yourself in the position to have an accurate view of who God is and what He's promised.

"God is utterly trustworthy, and with that we can be satisfied." –Hank Hanegraaff

VANEETHA: "HOW COULD GOD DO THIS?"

"One thing I'd thought before our son died was if you live right, God's going to do well by you. I thought for God to love me meant He was going to save my loved one. When Paul died, that sort of shattered. It felt so unfair. I had been faithful to God. How could God do this? I had begged God not to let my son die, and God did."

When we go through major suffering, we cry out, "Why?" and our beliefs about God can come into question. Put yourself in the position to find out the truth about who God is and whether He can be trusted. This is key to finding healing and comfort. This week's study will show you how to do that.

 DAY 1

Being real with God
"To lament is basically to say to God, 'Let me tell You where I am right now.'"
–Dr. Larry Crabb

GOD'S MESSAGE TO YOU
"I prayed, with hands lifted toward heaven, but my soul was not comforted. I think of God, and I moan, overwhelmed with longing for his help. You don't let me sleep. I am too distressed even to pray!

"I think of the good old days, long since ended, when my nights were filled with joyful songs. I search my soul and ponder the difference now. Has the Lord rejected me forever? ... Have his promises permanently failed?" (Psalm 77:2b–8 NLT)

1. Why do you think God wants you to know that godly people have cried out to Him and felt as if He wasn't listening?

2. Have you avoided being completely honest with God about your grief? If so, why?

3. What, if anything, has disappointed you about the amount of comfort you've received from God?

CONSIDER THIS

"Lamenting is a very healthy thing to do. As I lament, I'm pouring out my heart to God, and it is an action of worship, because I only cry out to people who I really believe can do something about it."
–Dr. Stephen Viars

Go through your workbook and use the laments found in the Psalms as your personal prayers.

TALKING TO GOD

Lord, thank you for letting me be honest with You. I have so much pain and confusion, and there's nowhere else to turn. Help me understand who You are and what You're doing.

DAY 2

I need to know Why!
God doesn't answer all our questions. Some things we're just not going to know. We have to be okay with that.

GOD'S MESSAGE TO YOU
"The secret things belong to the LORD our God, but the things revealed belong to us and to our children forever, that we may follow all the words of this law." (Deuteronomy 29:29)

1. What questions have you been repeating to God that you don't have answers to?

2. Why do you think God wants you to know there are some things He's chosen not to reveal to you?

3. Based on Deuteronomy 29:29, what is God's motivation for revealing truth to you?

CONSIDER THIS

"I can either put my focus on the answers God has already given me, or I can put my focus on the one ['why'] question that's not answered in the Scripture, and, therefore, ignore all the value He's given me in the Word." –Dr. Stephen Viars

TALKING TO GOD

God, help me to accept the fact that You're not going to answer all of my questions. Help me to value, even treasure, the answers You have shared with me. Give me the strength to put Your words into action, obeying what You command and trusting Your ways, so I might experience Your comfort.

DAY 3

I still need to know Why!
The details of God's plans are way too much for us to comprehend. And would we really want to trust in a God who can be fully understood by mere man? Or would we rather trust in a God who is powerful enough to deliver on what He's promised?

GOD'S MESSAGE TO YOU
"LORD, my heart is not proud; my eyes are not haughty. I don't concern myself with matters too great or too awesome for me to grasp. Instead, I have calmed and quieted myself, like a weaned child who no longer cries for its mother's milk. Yes, like a weaned child is my soul within me." (Psalm 131:1–2 NLT)

1. What is the difference between asking God questions and demanding answers?

2. What evidence does the psalmist give that he is not proud (see Psalm 131:1–2)?

3. How does it strike you that it could be considered prideful to demand answers from God?

"It felt so unfair." –Vaneetha

4. What kind of attitude should you have as you pursue God for answers to your "why" questions?

"God hates death. God says, 'It's wrong; it stinks; it wasn't supposed to be this way.' God is saying, 'I have a plan that will bless you and help you. And I have not ignored your loved one.'" –Susan Lutz

TALKING TO GOD

God, it feels like answers to my "why" questions would help me heal. Help me to remember that's not necessarily true. Please make it easier for me to recognize my limitations. And make me willing to accept the answers You have given regarding the whys of suffering and death.

DAY 4 — Do I have wrong assumptions about God?

Before your loved one died, you had certain beliefs about God and His role in people's lives. Now your beliefs have been put to the test, putting you in a position of

a. turning from God and trying to control life on your own;

b. trusting in what you've always believed to be true about God;

c. finding out the truth of who God is and whether He can be trusted.

GOD'S MESSAGE TO YOU

"[The LORD] said to Eliphaz the Temanite, 'I am angry with you and your two friends, because you have not spoken the truth about me, as my servant Job has.'" (Job 42:7b)

Jesus helps us know exactly what God is like: "[God] has spoken to us through his Son … The Son radiates God's own glory and expresses the very character of God." (Hebrews 1:2b–3a NLT)

1. In Job 42:7b, God is angry at Job's friends because they didn't speak the truth about Him. On a scale of 1–10, how sure are you that your beliefs about God and how He operates are accurate (1 being uncertain about the accuracy of your beliefs, and 10 being completely sure your beliefs are accurate)?

1 2 3 4 5 6 7 8 9 10

2. According to Hebrews 1:2b–3a, how does looking at Jesus's life help you to have an accurate view of what God is like?

3. What will you do to find out the truth of who God is?

"We may not get direct answers to our questions on this side of life, but the answers reside in who God is in His character, in what we know to be true about God." –Dr. Joseph Stowell

TALKING TO GOD

God, I need to know who You really are, what You're doing, and whether You can be trusted. Help me to open my ears and hear what You are saying to me.

DAY 5 — The key to healing and hope

The more you understand about God's character, the more progress you'll make in your healing.

"I don't want suffering, but suffering has done the deepest work in my life." –Vaneetha

GOD'S MESSAGE TO YOU

"Then Job replied to the LORD: 'I know that you can do all things; no purpose of yours can be thwarted. You asked, "Who is this that obscures my plans without knowledge?" Surely I spoke of things I did not understand, things too wonderful for me to know … My ears had heard of you but now my eyes have seen you.'" (Job 42:1–5)

1. After the death of his children and the loss of his livelihood, health, and possessions, Job questioned God. But after Job's lamenting, what does he realize about God (see Job 42:1–5)?

2. How has your view of God changed since your loved one's death?

3. What does Job realize about himself (see Job 42:1–5)?*

* Read page xii to find out how God can be your loving Savior and comforter in the midst of deep pain and suffering.

CONSIDER THIS

"The Bible presents God as One who is completely sovereign over the affairs of men. And that's the kind of God I want to trust. Because if He's sovereign over my life today, that means He can be sovereign over my life in eternity." –Dr. Stephen Viars

God has not forgotten you, nor your loved one. He has a plan and purpose that is good and that is still being played out.

TALKING TO GOD

God, I want to rest in Your perfect plan for my life, my loved ones' lives, and for eternity.
Help me to trust You.

VANEETHA: LOOKING BACK

"There's an incredible comfort in knowing that I'll see [my son] again, but also the fact that there will be no more suffering, no more tears, and no more pain. God has the opportunity then to show me how He's redeemed everything that I've been through. Some of the things that seem so hard now, that we never get answers for, we'll see the bigger picture there [in heaven]."*

* The Natalie Grant song "Held" was written based on Vaneetha's story of the death of her infant son.

NEXT SESSION
Learn what to do with regrets, guilt, bitterness, and anger.

FREE DAILY EMAIL ENCOURAGEMENT

SIGN UP FOR "A SEASON OF GRIEF." RECEIVE AN UPLIFTING EMAIL MESSAGE EACH DAY FOR A YEAR.

"I look for the wonderful, inspirational messages I get from you in the morning. Your thoughts are much better than what runs through my head during this time."

"They helped me through despair, anxiety, many tearful days."

GRIEFSHARE.ORG/MY

GRIEF SHARE

"It's such a huge shift in my understanding of God." –Vaneetha

MY WEEKLY GRIEF WORK

Session – Six

PERSONAL CHECKUP – TRACK YOUR HEALING PROGRESS

Place a check in the box identifying how you're feeling. Insert words to explain why.

	REALLY BAD	OKAY	PRETTY GOOD	GREAT
EMOTIONALLY				
PHYSICALLY				
SPIRITUALLY				
RELATIONALLY				

JOURNAL TOPICS – MAKING SENSE OF IT ALL

Choose the idea below, or choose your own topic. We encourage you to use a separate notebook for your weekly journaling.

This week you learned about the importance of lamenting. Use your journal to cry out to God with all the questions, hurt, anger, and confusion that is plaguing you.

MOVING FORWARD – PRACTICAL STEPS TOWARD HEALING
HOW TO DEAL WITH ALL YOUR QUESTIONS
"I have calmed and quieted myself." (Psalm 131:2a NLT)

Listed below are practical things you can do to "calm and quiet yourself" when you're stressed. Mark one or two to try out this week. Underneath, write how you plan to implement those ideas.

- ○ Make a to-do list with three items each day, and only concentrate on one at a time.
- ○ Exercise.
- ○ Eat healthy food.
- ○ Don't look too far into the future. Focus on today.

- ○ Write in your journal.
- ○ Talk with others.
- ○ Meditate on Scripture.
- ○ Pray.
- ○ Trust that God has provided you with the resources to handle your new normal, instead of focusing on where you feel inadequate.

Plans to put into action:

_____

_____

GUILT AND ANGER

"If only I had insisted he stay home."
"I knew I should have taken her to a different doctor."
"Why didn't I tell him, 'I'm sorry'?"

Regret, guilt, and anger are three emotions that can create barriers against the peace and healing God has for you. If you're facing these obstacles or others, Session 7 will help you to overcome them.

By viewing the video, being part of the small group discussion, and completing the **FROM MOURNING TO JOY** exercises, you'll learn how to:

 Deal with false guilt

Grieve conflicted relationships

Handle grief-related anger

VIDEO OUTLINE

Use this outline to write down important concepts, encouraging words, or questions you have while viewing the video.

SOURCES OF FALSE GUILT

What ifs

AVOIDING FALSE GUILT

Was it your fault?

"God knows the exact time we will die. There's nothing you can do to extend your lifespan one-tenth of a second." –Zig Ziglar

God has numbered our days   (Psalm 139:16)

It's okay to heal

Phoebe's story

TRUE GUILT

Unresolved conflict

Seek forgiveness

ANGER & GRIEF

A painful combination

Forgive   (Ephesians 4:32, Romans 12:19)

"The only way we can [forgive] people is by remembering Christ has forgiven us." –Elyse Fitzpatrick

Blaming God

Is it okay to be angry at God?

Keep talking to God

In this week's From Mourning to Joy exercises ...
Joanne experienced great anger, unforgiveness, and guilt after her son's death. This week's exercises will give you tools to deal with these tough emotions.

"Anger at God is fueled by a sense of entitlement." –Phil Sasser

WHY SHOULD I FORGIVE?

Forgiveness makes more sense when, instead of focusing on the wrong done to you, you think about God's character and the manner in which He forgave you. Here's a story that Jesus told to encourage you to forgive.

AN ABUNDANCE OF FORGIVENESS

"Therefore, the Kingdom of Heaven can be compared to a king who decided to bring his accounts up to date with servants who had borrowed money from him. In the process, one of his debtors was brought in who owed him millions of dollars. He couldn't pay, so his master ordered that he be sold—along with his wife, his children, and everything he owned—to pay the debt.

"But the man fell down before his master and begged him, 'Please, be patient with me, and I will pay it all.' Then his master was filled with pity for him, and he released him and forgave his debt.

AN ABSENCE OF MERCY

"But when the man left the king, he went to a fellow servant who owed him a few thousand dollars. He grabbed him by the throat and demanded instant payment. His fellow servant fell down before him and begged for a little more time. 'Be patient with me, and I will pay it,' he pleaded. But his creditor wouldn't wait. He had the man arrested and put in prison until the debt could be paid in full.

AN AROUSAL OF ANGER

"When some of the other servants saw this, they were very upset. They went to the king and told him everything that had happened. Then the king called in the man he had forgiven and said, 'You evil servant! I forgave you that tremendous debt because you pleaded with me. Shouldn't you have mercy on your fellow servant, just as I had mercy on you?' Then the angry king sent the man to prison to be tortured until he had paid his entire debt.

"That's what my heavenly Father will do to you if you refuse to forgive your brothers and sisters from your heart." (Matthew 18:23–35 NLT)

Lorraine Peterson explains, "God is perfect and He forgave me. Who am I to say, 'I'm not going to forgive that other person; he doesn't deserve it.' I didn't deserve to be forgiven by God. That person gets my forgiveness whether or not he deserves it."

AN ABSENCE OF JUSTICE?

Sorting out the emotions of grief is complicated. It's complicated even further when your loved one's death occurred because of someone's negligence or violence. If that's your situation, know that God cares for you and invites you to find comfort in Him and in the fact that one day He'll put an end to all suffering and punish all injustice. But in the midst of your pain and confusion, remember that it's very important for you to forgive. Jesus says, "But if you do not forgive others their sins, your Father will not forgive your sins" (Matthew 6:15). We forgive because we've been forgiven.

To learn more about how to experience God's forgiveness, see the article in the front of your workbook entitled "God, What Is Going On?"

FROM MOURNING TO JOY

ENCOURAGEMENT AND COMFORT FROM GOD'S WORD

Session Seven – Guilt and Anger

JOANNE: "I SWORE I'D NEVER FORGIVE"

Joanne's son died in a car accident. He was a passenger in a vehicle that hit a weed-sprayer truck parked on the roadside. "I swore I would never forgive the person who was driving the car or the guy who had the weed-sprayer on the side of the road who wasn't doing his job according to the law. I also believed my son was taken from me because of sins I had committed, my actions, and my lack of faith in God. I was angry. I was unforgiving."

You might be feeling angry and bitter over what has happened. Perhaps you are struggling with guilt, with "If onlys." These emotions can block your healing process and need to be addressed. This week we'll continue our discussion on how to take care of difficult emotions.

DAY 1

Feelings of guilt
"If only ... What if ..." These thoughts can plague a person in grief. How do you get rid of them?

GOD'S MESSAGE TO YOU

"You [God] saw me before I was born. Every day of my life was recorded in your book. Every moment was laid out before a single day had passed." (Psalm 139:16 NLT)

1. What struggles do you have with "If onlys" and feelings of guilt about your actions/decisions surrounding your loved one's death?

2. According to Psalm 139:16, when was it decided how many days you and your loved one would live?

3. Write your thoughts and questions about Psalm 139:16 in a prayer to God below.

CONSIDER THIS

"Psalm 139:16 clearly states that our life every day is measured, meaning simply–God knows the exact time that we will die. He knows when He's going to call us home. There's nothing you can do to extend your life span [or someone else's] one-tenth of a second."
–Zig Ziglar

TALKING TO GOD

God, I give my feelings of guilt, my "If onlys," to You. I lay them at Your feet because they are too heavy a burden to carry. It was my loved one's time to go. Please comfort me in my pain.

"We make the best decisions we can at the time, and sometimes the outcomes are not good." –Bryan

DAY 2 — Desiring justice, or revenge?

What do you think the Bible says about justice and revenge when someone has sinned against you or your loved one?

GOD'S MESSAGE TO YOU

"Do not take revenge, my dear friends, but leave room for God's wrath, for it is written: 'It is mine to avenge; I will repay,' says the Lord." (Romans 12:19)

"God is just: He will pay back trouble to those who trouble you." (2 Thessalonians 1:6)

1. Perhaps you have desired revenge or payback from someone who has wronged you. What has God promised you in Romans 12:19 and 2 Thessalonians 1:6?

2. Our attempts at taking revenge never ultimately satisfy. According to 2 Thessalonians 1:6, how do you know that God will not let a wrong go unpunished?

3. Instead of occupying your time with blame or revenge, what could you do with your time that would honor your lost loved one and honor God?

CONSIDER THIS

"God has committed Himself to exact justice on this person at a level that's far more thorough than a human criminal justice system." –Susan Lutz

TALKING TO GOD

God, sometimes my blame and anger fuel me, and I keep fanning the flames in my mind. I don't want to continue to live in this nightmarish place of vengeance–and I don't have to. Right now, I surrender it to You. Help me to trust You to bring about justice.

DAY 3 — What does it mean to forgive?

Forgive? No way. Forgiveness can seem impossible, but it is a crucial part of healing. Refusing to forgive blocks your healing and shapes you into a person you don't want to be.

GOD'S MESSAGE TO YOU

"Forgive as the Lord forgave you." (Colossians 3:13b)

"For if you forgive other people when they sin against you, your heavenly Father will also forgive you. But if you do not forgive others their sins, your Father will not forgive your sins." (Matthew 6:14–15)

1. Whom do you struggle to forgive, and why?

2. According to Colossians 3:13b, how are we to forgive?

3. When does God withhold forgiveness from you (see Matthew 6:14–15)?

"It is mine to avenge; I will repay." –God (Romans 12:19)

CONSIDER THIS

What the Bible teaches about forgiveness:

- Forgiveness doesn't mean you condone what the person did or that you trust the person.

- Forgiveness is about getting your heart right with God. It is foremost about your relationship with God.

- It frees you from a lifetime of bondage to a bitter and hardened heart.

- Forgiveness isn't a one-time act. You'll have to continue to choose forgiveness.

- We forgive because God has forgiven us.

- Forgiveness doesn't mean you're letting the other person off the hook. It's entrusting God to take care of the situation for you.

- Forgiveness isn't reconciliation. Reconciliation requires genuine repentance on the part of the person who was wrong.

If you want to forgive, don't focus on what's been done to you. Focus on what you've done to God and the fact that He's forgiven you (see this week's Day 5 and the article on page 66).

TALKING TO GOD

God, I can't do this on my own. Forgiveness seems impossible, but I want to do it. I don't want to turn into a bitter, unloving person. Help me to understand just how much You've forgiven me.

 DAY 4 **Anger with God**
Maybe you're not angry with another person, but with God.

GOD'S MESSAGE TO YOU
Job was a man faithful to God who experienced great loss and suffering. At one point he questioned and complained to God. The book of Job explains what happened next ...

"Then the LORD spoke to Job out of the storm: 'Brace yourself like a man; I will question you, and you shall answer me. Would you discredit my justice? Would you condemn me to justify yourself?'" (Job 40:6–8)

1. Rate your level of anger with God (1 being not angry, 10 being extremely angry):

1 2 3 4 5 6 7 8 9 10

2. Is your anger causing you to (check the following that apply):

○ Not want to pray
○ Not want to go to church
○ Not want to read your Bible
○ Reject the goodness of God
○ Close your ears to His voice

3. It's right for us to think of God as loving and patient. But Job 40:6–8 shows us that God also demands reverence and respect. How have you shown God that you respect and revere Him as you've processed your grief emotions? How could you improve in this area?

CONSIDER THIS

Anger with God is always the result of a conclusion that a perfect God has treated you unjustly. But we don't have the right to judge God. Thankfully, He understands your pain and frustration.

Take your heartfelt anger and pain to the Lord, while holding on to the truths you know about Him. He is trustworthy and faithful; He has not wronged you. He loves you, and He proved it at the cross.

Read more about how God proved His love for you on page xii.

"I had so much anger built up in me." –Joanne

God, I've been accusing You of things I know nothing about. You are God, and Your good plan and Your perfect ways are beyond my comprehension. Someday I might understand, but for now, help me trust You.

DAY 5 — You can be forgiven

Maybe you struggle because you behaved or treated someone wrongly, whether before or since the death, and you feel badly about it. And if it was toward your loved one, you wonder what can even be done about it?

God offers you a place of rest and forgiveness.

GOD'S MESSAGE TO YOU

"He has removed our sins as far from us as the east is from the west." (Psalm 103:12 NLT)

"If you, LORD, kept a record of sins ... who could stand? But with you there is forgiveness." (Psalm 130:3–4a)

1. If you've confessed your sins to Christ and have believed in what He's done for you, how far away are your sins from you (see Psalm 103:12)?

2. How thorough is God's forgiveness (see Psalm 103:12)?

3. According to Psalm 130:3–4a, who needs forgiveness?

4. If you truly believe the truths of today's Bible verses, in addition to feeling sorrow over sin what other emotions do you feel as you contemplate your forgiveness?

CONSIDER THIS

"If you say, 'I know that God forgives me, but I can't forgive myself,' you're underestimating what it cost God to forgive you. You're removing yourself from the greatest blessing of life and you are saying, 'My standards are more important.'" –Susan Lutz

TALKING TO GOD

God, it's so hard not to keep condemning myself, but I choose instead to receive Your forgiveness and to trust that Your forgiveness is perfect and complete. I can rest in that forgiveness and not try to place my own standards above Yours.

JOANNE: LOOKING BACK

"After I came to the Lord, I realized, 'If He could forgive, then surely I could forgive.' It took a long time, but I realized I needed to do that. I also realized that Kyle didn't die because of my sins, and I started to feel a lot of that guilt being relieved. Forgiving has relieved a very heavy load off my shoulders. Every human is not perfect. I'm not perfect. I realized that could have been me driving that truck. Forgiveness is definitely a process."

NEXT SESSION
Learn how to deal with problems that are complicating your grief.

MY WEEKLY GRIEF WORK

Session - Seven

PERSONAL CHECKUP – TRACK YOUR HEALING PROGRESS
Place a check in the box identifying how you're feeling. Insert words to explain why.

	REALLY BAD	OKAY	PRETTY GOOD	GREAT
EMOTIONALLY				
PHYSICALLY				
SPIRITUALLY				
RELATIONALLY				

JOURNAL TOPICS – MAKING SENSE OF IT ALL
Choose one or more ideas below, or choose your own topic. We encourage
you to use a separate notebook for your weekly journaling.

✎ Write a prayer to God explaining why you don't want to forgive someone and asking for His help. Describe how unforgiveness is harming you and those around you.

✎ What concerns do you have about unfinished business between you and your loved one? Bring these concerns to God.

MOVING FORWARD – PRACTICAL STEPS TOWARD HEALING
HOW TO DEAL WITH GUILT
Completing the chart on the next page will help you face and evaluate feelings of guilt over past actions/
decisions in order to meet the present and future with freedom and assurance.

Column 1: Describe a past experience you feel guilty about.

Column 2: Describe your inner and outer response to your guilt.

Column 3: Find out what God's Word says about it. *(Consider truths you've learned so far in GriefShare. Ask your GriefShare leader, church leaders, or Christian friends to direct you to applicable biblical truths.)*

Column 4: Record what you'll do next as a result of what you've learned, in order to bring about change.

My Responses to Guilt

I FEEL GUILTY ABOUT	HOW I'VE RESPONDED	WHAT GOD'S WORD SAYS	WHAT I'LL DO THE NEXT TIME I FEEL GUILTY

"GOD CAN BOTH FORGIVE YOU AND COMFORT YOU." —BRAD HAMBRICK

CONTINUE HEALING WITH

MyGriefShare+

Your personal library of GriefShare videos

$25 annual subscription

What is MyGriefShare+?

MyGriefShare+ is a library of hundreds of additional grief-related videos designed to help you continue healing during your GriefShare group and after it ends.

With this annual subscription service, you can:

- Access 200+ videos essential to your healing
- Get more advice from popular GriefShare experts & testimonials
- Find answers to the questions you have about your grief
- Learn more about your grief by watching previous editions of GriefShare

Get continued support after your group sessions end–subscribe today!

NEW CONTENT ADDED MONTHLY

Subscribe or learn more at

GRIEFSHARE.ORG/PLUS

COMPLICATING FACTORS

8
SESSION

IT'S BEEN WEEKS SINCE YOU'VE SLEPT THROUGH THE NIGHT.
You can't remember the last time you smiled. And you can't concentrate long enough to follow a box-mix, blueberry muffin recipe. Grief can be complicated, and it is relentless. Not only do you have to deal with the pain of your loved one being gone, but you face many other symptoms day and night that people around you don't realize you're struggling with.

By viewing the video, being part of the small group discussion, and completing the **FROM MOURNING TO JOY** exercises, you'll begin to see:

 How traumatic experiences affect grief

How to deal with nightmares and flashbacks

How your thinking affects your emotions

VIDEO OUTLINE

Use this outline to write down important concepts, encouraging words, or questions you have while viewing the video.

TRAUMA

Its effect on grief

TRAUMA SYMPTOMS

Flashbacks

"A great way to deal with trauma is by staying in the present." –David Bueno Martin

Dealing with flashbacks

Nightmares

TRAUMA & MULTIPLE DEATHS

Grieve each loss

Share your story

TRAUMA OF SUICIDE

Shame

Share your pain

"Is my loved one in heaven?"

TRAUMA OF MURDER

Unique challenges

Go to God

"When you share that shame and guilt in community, that helps you heal." –David Bueno Martin

Soil for healing   (Proverbs 23:7)

Destructive thoughts

Destructive Thoughts

"God's not good"

"God's not loving"

"God's not powerful"

"It's my fault"

"Life is meaningless"

"I can't do this"

"I'm all alone"

"There's no hope"

Self-talk   (Philippians 4:19, Psalm 43:5)

In this week's From Mourning to Joy exercises ...

Iris came to a negative conclusion about the circumstances leading up to the deaths, that she convinced herself was true. Find out how to control your negative self-talk and replace it with truth, which leads to hope.

"You want to tell yourself truth." –Julie Ganschow

POST-TRAUMATIC STRESS DISORDER

Sometimes traumatic experiences can leave you suffering from what medical professionals call post-traumatic stress disorder, or PTSD. How do you know if you're suffering from PTSD? Only a doctor can tell you that. But we asked psychiatrist Dr. Avak Albert Howsepian and certified trauma specialist H. Norman Wright to share with us some common symptoms.

Q: What type of experience would be considered a traumatic experience that could result in PTSD?

Dr. Howsepian: To have post-traumatic stress disorder, [you must have been exposed to] a traumatic experience, which is an experience that involves an exposure to death, or the threat of death, or serious injury, or sexual assault. Those kinds of things can be experienced in multiple ways. One might be the victim of an assault or a threat of death. One might be a witness, seeing someone else assaulted or someone else die. Or someone might hear about the death of someone by way of a violent act or an accident, or learn in intimate detail aspects of someone else having been traumatized in some way; that counts as a traumatic experience.

Q: What are some common symptoms of PTSD?

Dr. Howsepian: The symptoms of PTSD that complicate normal grief include flashback experiences, nightmares, avoidance of reminders of the trauma, negative changes in someone's mood or how they think about themselves or the world, not being able to relax easily, not being able to concentrate, difficulty sleeping, startling very easily, feeling irritable and aggressive. These symptoms have to last at least one month, and they have to be significantly distressing to the individual or interfere significantly with some important aspects of their life.

H. Norman Wright: Disruptive sleeping patterns, tremendous irritability, snapping at people, and impatience. Hypervigilance, where you're really on edge and you're scanning the environment. Intrusive thoughts, where all of a sudden that thought comes in and you're replaying it in your mind. You also have what we call the startle response, where a sound or a sight can trigger you because it's reflective of what you experienced, the screeching of brakes, the dropping of books on the floor with kids in school and it sounds like a gun going off again.

Q: What are some differences between symptoms of bereavement and symptoms of PTSD?

Dr. Howsepian: Symptoms more central to post-traumatic stress disorder than to bereavement: aggression, self-destructive activity or thoughts, and fear about feeling safe in the world.

Q: Why are some people embarrassed to admit they have PTSD?

Dr. Howsepian: PTSD has, in many respects, a significant social stigma, in part because the person [doesn't] have injuries that others can readily see. With PTSD it appears as if the individuals who claim to be suffering from that condition have nothing wrong with them at all; they seem in every respect quite healthy. So one might attribute their PTSD to

a certain kind of internal weakness that they might have and stigmatize them for that reason. This becomes all the more important in the context of combat where individuals are expected to act in a way that's quite courageous, to be in control, and to be strong. And then in that context if someone suffers a trauma that results in PTSD, they might even think of themselves as having been a coward or having been weak.

Q: Can a person recover from PTSD?

Dr. Howsepian: Most people with PTSD resolve their PTSD. It's only a minority of PTSD cases that become chronic, so the brain can heal, and in most cases it does heal to some degree. And if we take the notion of post-traumatic growth seriously, there are times when the brain heals in a way that's even better, more robust, and stronger than it was prior to the trauma.

If you think you're suffering from PTSD, don't feel ashamed. Find help. Reach out to your doctor or a Christian psychologist or Christian psychiatrist to find help.

IRIS: "NOTHING GOOD HAPPENS"

Iris's mom died from complications due to alcoholism. Iris's experience affected her view of herself and God. "I was nineteen years old and I would be like, 'Mom, can you stop? You're going to kill yourself.' It was like talking to a wall. I felt like I wasn't worth it for her to live. The same thing with my boyfriend, I'm like, 'Stop doing what you're doing.' If I was worth it, he would [stop]." Instead, he ended up getting murdered. "I feel like I pray, and nothing good happens. Everything you can think of bad has happened to me. So I'm to the point, 'Why would God love me? He don't love me.'"

Like Iris, you're drawing conclusions about your situation. Your tendency will be to repeat them in your mind to the point that they affect the way you think about God and your expectations for the future. This is why it's important that you draw accurate conclusions about your grief experience. Otherwise, negative self-talk will deepen your negative emotions and keep you from having peace and hope. This week you'll learn how to monitor your thinking, renew your mind, and experience hope.

DAY 1

A peace that transcends understanding

"Peace" is not just a warm, content feeling. The Bible talks about a peace that is able to protect your heart and your thoughts.

GOD'S MESSAGE TO YOU

"Do not be anxious about anything, but in every situation, by prayer and petition, with thanksgiving, present your requests to God. And the peace of God, which transcends all understanding, will guard your hearts and your minds in Christ Jesus." (Philippians 4:6–7)

1. According to Philippians 4:6–7, which situations, worries, and concerns in our life are we to bring to God?

2. What is the result of consistently choosing to trust God with your anxieties (see Philippians 4:6–7)?

3. What requests do you have for God right now?

CONSIDER THIS

"How can I not be anxious?

- *I make a decision not to be anxious.*
- *I take [my anxieties to God] with great intentionality, focus, and determination.*
- *I just keep coming back and coming back.*
- *I thank Him ahead of time for the outcome.*

"God says, 'I promise I will protect you both mentally and emotionally.'" –Dr. Crawford Loritts

TALKING TO GOD

God, help me to bring my anxieties to You as soon as they surface, choosing this positive step instead of wallowing in worries. Please protect my mind and my heart with Your peace by keeping me in close connection with Christ.

 DAY 2 **What are you focusing on?**
How to experience peace: focused reliance upon the Lord.

GOD'S MESSAGE TO YOU
"You [God] will keep in perfect peace all who trust in you, all whose thoughts are fixed on you!" (Isaiah 26:3 NLT)

1. What types of negative thoughts have been recurrent for you?

2. According to Isaiah 26:3, how do you find rest and peace?

3. Write ideas of ways to keep your thoughts fixed on God.

CONSIDER THIS

"Whenever my mind is really on Jesus, it can't be in turmoil; peace will come. The problem is learning how to stay our minds on Jesus, but there's a goal there, and we need to reach for it." –Lorraine Peterson

TALKING TO GOD

God, I can't keep my thoughts fixed on You without Your help. Again and again, as my focus wanders down paths that are unhealthy, please direct me back to Your promises and Your love.

 DAY 3 **Monitor your thinking**
Find out how to take control of your thoughts.

GOD'S MESSAGE TO YOU
"We take captive [bring under control] every thought to make it obedient to Christ." (2 Corinthians 10:5b)

"Blessed is the one ... whose delight is in the law of the LORD, and who meditates on his law [God's words in the Bible] day and night." (Psalm 1:1–2)

1. Based on 2 Corinthians 10:5b, what can you do with thoughts that are contrary to God's truth?

2. To control negative self-talk, you have to counter it with God's truth. For instance, if you feel alone, you have to remind yourself **the truth is** God says He is with me (Psalm 34:18). If you are inappropriately blaming yourself for the death, remind yourself **the truth is** God determined how long my loved one would live (Psalm 139:16). What can you do to remind yourself what God says is true about your situation?

3. One way to keep God's truth on your mind is to *meditate* on Scripture. To meditate means to reflect upon or contemplate. Based upon Psalm 1:1–2, how often does the psalmist meditate on God's Word?

"God created us with more than our emotions." –Dr. Stephen Viars

"If I allow myself to think, 'No one can relate to this. I'm really alone in this,' that's a lie. The truth is, God can equip other people to care for us." –Carla

TALKING TO GOD

God, my negative self-talk can really bring me down. Help me to speak truth to myself, Your truth. I want to get into Your Word and learn what truth really is.

CHARACTERISTICS OF NEGATIVE SELF-TALK

- It's not true.
- It does not build you up or help you grow.
- It exaggerates the impact and extent of legitimate problems.

DAY 4

Renewing your mind

Change comes when we renew the way we think. When we renew the way we think, we see things from a different perspective.

GOD'S MESSAGE TO YOU
"Do not conform to the pattern of this world, but be transformed by the renewing of your mind. Then you will be able to test and approve what God's will is–his good, pleasing and perfect will." (Romans 12:2)

1. Which thought pattern sounds more like you?

○ I miss my loved one so much. I cannot possibly go on. It's the end of the world for me.

○ I miss my loved one so much. I'm not sure how I'm going to be able to cope, but with God's help I can make it through each day one painful step at a time.

2. In order to renew your mind, or transform the way you think, you need to look at the situation from a different perspective, in light of the bigger picture of eternity and in light of God's truth.

Write down a feeling you've been struggling with on the lines below.

I feel _____ because _____
_____

On the next line, prayerfully write down a truth from God that you've learned.

But, the truth is, _____
_____

CONSIDER THIS

"When I have irrational, disturbing, negative thoughts, I can replace them with the truth of God in His Word."
–Dr. Elias Moitinho

TALKING TO GOD

God, please help me day by day to renew my mind by reading Your Word and by applying it to my negative thinking.

DAY 5

Finding hope

Hope does not come from getting better, but from getting to know God better and learning what His plan is for eternity.

GOD'S MESSAGE TO YOU
"For everything that was written in the past was written to teach us, so that through the endurance taught in the Scriptures and the encouragement they provide we might have hope." (Romans 15:4)

1. Romans 15:4 shares two things that work together to bring hope. Fill in the blanks below.

_____ + _____ = Hope

"There are some things that just aren't productive to think about." –Bryan

2. Based upon the truths presented in Romans 15:4, what practical steps can you take to produce hope?

CONSIDER THIS

"Our whole relationship with the Lord is based on the fact that the good hope—the hope that we know where we're going, we know what's been done for us— is what keeps us going because we know the accomplished end." –David

"Immerse yourself in the Word. Find out that God really does intend all of these things, ultimately, to come together for your good." –Dr. Robert DeVries

TALKING TO GOD

God, I want to have Your kind of hope for my daily life. Help me to remember that You promise something better than what I feel and see around me.

IRIS: LOOKING BACK

"Reading God's Word has helped me out a lot. It helps me understand more about life, what to expect out of God, and what God needs to expect out of you; how to deal with issues, pain, [and] suffering; and why God would take you through so much stuff in your lifetime. He brings you closer to Him basically. I feel everything I've been through has just brought me closer to God. The more I trust God, the more I see Him coming through for me, which makes me want to trust God more."

NEXT SESSION
Discover how to avoid becoming stuck in grief.

"It's important to speak the truth despite how you feel." –Dr. Crawford Loritts

MY WEEKLY GRIEF WORK

Session - Eight

PERSONAL CHECKUP - TRACK YOUR HEALING PROGRESS
Place a check in the box identifying how you're feeling. Insert words to explain why.

	REALLY BAD	OKAY	PRETTY GOOD	GREAT
EMOTIONALLY				
PHYSICALLY				
SPIRITUALLY				
RELATIONALLY				

JOURNAL TOPICS - MAKING SENSE OF IT ALL
Choose one or more ideas below, or choose your own topic. We encourage
you to use a separate notebook for your weekly journaling.

✎ Write a (non-mailed) letter to the person you are angry at. Give these emotions to God.

✎ If you're having trouble getting a negative image of your loved one's death out of your mind, think of a beautiful, precious memory of your loved one to replace it. Describe this positive memory/image of your loved one in great detail.

MOVING FORWARD - PRACTICAL STEPS TOWARD HEALING
HOW TO RECOGNIZE AND CORRECT WRONG THINKING
Meditating on Scripture (reflecting on what the Bible says) will equip you with God's truths to counter wrong thinking patterns. Below are some questions that will help you meditate on a verse of Scripture. You can use these questions for any Bible verses you choose. (Or, for this week, we suggest you read Psalm 139. When you're done, reflect on the chapter using the questions below as prompts.)

1. What promises are in these verses?

2. Why would God want me to know what's in the passage I just read?

3. How is what I've read contrary to the way I tend to think?

4. What do these verses reveal about God's character?

5. What would it look like if I applied the truths in this passage, or obeyed what it's instructing me to do?

STUCK

SESSION

IF YOU'RE NOT CAREFUL, THREE TO FIVE YEARS FROM NOW your grief can be just as intense and raw as it is right now. Some people call that being stuck in grief. This session offers preventative measures you can take to ensure that you don't get stuck and that you're grieving in a way that leads to healing.

As you view the video and complete your **FROM MOURNING TO JOY** and **MY WEEKLY GRIEF WORK** exercises, you'll find out:

 How to prevent getting stuck in grief

Common misconceptions that hinder healing

Why your path to healing isn't always smooth

VIDEO OUTLINE

Use this outline to write down important concepts, encouraging words, or questions you have while viewing the video.

NORMAL OR STUCK?

The differences   (Ecclesiastes 3:4)

BELIEF TUNE-UP

"Time heals"

"Stay busy"

"Everything we say is ours really is on loan to us." –Dr. Crawford Loritts

GRIEF SHARE

SESSION NINE Stuck

85

"I'm *the* caregiver"

"God took *my* loved one"   (Job 1:21)

"Healing = forgetting"

"Progress is steady"

God & your situation

GETTING UNSTUCK

Do your grief work

Don't obey your feelings   (Luke 22:42)

Worship God   (Psalm 63:3–4, Job 1:20–21)

"We can't let our emotions drive the train during our time of grief." –Dr. Joseph Stowell

Be grateful   (1 Thessalonians 5:18)

Put God on display   (1 Thessalonians 4:13)

In this week's From Mourning to Joy exercises ...

You'll learn more about Bryan, whose daughter was murdered, and find out how he avoided becoming stuck in grief and how you can, too.

BRYAN: "AUSTIN WAS A GIFT FROM GOD"

"When we got to the classroom where Austin died, I sat down on the floor. I wanted to be in the spot she had last been alive. The thought that came to my mind was not how she died, but when she was first born. I had been standing in our backyard and [my pastor] had said, 'I want you to always remember that Austin is a gift from God.' That's what came into my mind as I sat there, that Austin was a gift from God, and now she had returned to God."

You saw on the video several beliefs that can get you stuck in grief, such as the belief that your loved ones belong to you instead of God. In this week's session you'll find encouragement to do your grief work and avoid becoming stuck in grief.

DAY 1

Walk by truth, not feelings
Don't let your feelings dictate how you think, act, and behave. Just because you feel something intensely doesn't make it right, true, or helpful.

GOD'S MESSAGE TO YOU
"God is our refuge and strength, an ever-present help in trouble." (Psalm 46:1)

"The instructions of the Lord are perfect, reviving the soul. The decrees of the Lord are trustworthy, making wise the simple." (Psalm 19:7 NLT)

"Trust in the LORD with all your heart and lean not on your own understanding." (Proverbs 3:5)

1. Sometimes, people get stuck in grief because they conclude God has abandoned them. Based on that conclusion, they feel reading God's Word won't help them. Yet that is contrary to Psalm 46:1, Psalm 19:7, and other Scriptures. According to Proverbs 3:5, what should you do when your understanding of your circumstances is in conflict with what God says?

2. Consider how you are thinking about (understanding) your circumstances–the conclusions you are drawing. Also consider how you are responding to those conclusions. In what ways do your conclusions and responses differ from what God's Word says?

This is what I think: _____

_____

In response to that understanding, I've been:

_____

This is what God's Word says about my conclusions and responses: _____

_____

"Truth is not dependent on feelings." –Connie

3. How can you demonstrate your belief that it's better to trust in the Lord than to lean on your own understanding (see Proverbs 3:5)?

CONSIDER THIS

"We can be honest about what we're feeling, but that doesn't mean we have to be driven by what we're feeling. If I wait around to do things based on how I feel, I'm going to be an absolute mess."
–Dr. Stephen Viars

TALKING TO GOD

God, it's hard to see through my tangled emotions, in order to believe and act on the truth of Your promises. Help me to take each step by faith, choosing to cling to what You've said is true.

 DAY 2 ## You have a purpose
There's a reason you're still alive.

GOD'S MESSAGE TO YOU
"For we are God's handiwork, created in Christ Jesus to do good works, which God prepared in advance for us to do." (Ephesians 2:10)

1. According to Ephesians 2:10, what did God create you to do?

2. Did your purpose for living cease with your loved one's death? Why or why not?

3. In order to do the good works God prepared specifically for you, you need to first do the grief work to help you heal. Write down a step you will commit to taking to do your grief work (perhaps a way to store memories, express your emotions, or develop a new normal).

CONSIDER THIS

"Doing grief work means rolling up your sleeves and doing the tough stuff. I would contend that if we don't do those tough things, we really won't ever completely heal." –Dr. Susan Zonnebelt-Smeenge

"My wife and I decided that we were going to spend our time more focused on service and outreach, because we thought that was a more likely path to healing." –Bryan

TALKING TO GOD

God, You have good works prepared for me to do. But first, I need to do my grief work, and I can't do it on my own. It's so hard. Please help me to step out and do the work, one day at a time.

 DAY 3 ## Worship looks different now
"In the midst of grief, worship looks different. The rawness of worship in the midst of grief will feel awkward." –Brad Hambrick

Yet, worship helps keep you from becoming stuck.

GOD'S MESSAGE TO YOU
"Job got up and tore his robe and shaved his head. Then he fell to the ground in worship and said: 'Naked I came from my mother's womb, and naked I will depart. The LORD gave and the LORD has taken away; may the name of the LORD be praised.'" (Job 1:20–21)

1. What does Job realize in Job 1:20–21 (after the death of his children and his many other losses)?

"Worship is relating to God with an accurate picture of who He is." –Brad Hambrick

2. Based on today's Bible passage, do we have to be happy to worship or praise God?

3. Even though you're probably sad, you can praise God right now. How? Simply write down a few things that God deserves to be praised for. Or, tell a friend or family member about a good thing God has done, or share something about God that you're thankful for.

CONSIDER THIS

"We brought nothing into this world. All that we have are gifts of God; the loved ones in our life are His gifts. Our response to His giving and to His taking away is that we will worship the Lord. He is worthy of praise."
–Phil Sasser

"I'm going to cry out to Him even when it's hard."
–Dr. Stephen Viars

TALKING TO GOD

God, thank you for the gift of my loved one, such a precious gift. Help me to understand that my time for having that gift is over, but my loved one and I are still part of a larger plan. I will worship You amid my tears because You are God.

DAY 4

Be thankful?
Being grateful helps you avoid becoming stuck. There's always something to be thankful for:

- The time I had with my loved one.
- I'll see my loved one again.
- My loved one is no longer suffering.
- What I've learned from my loved one.
- How God is helping me, comforting me, and providing for me in my grief.

GOD'S MESSAGE TO YOU
"Give thanks in all circumstances; for this is God's will for you in Christ Jesus." (1 Thessalonians 5:18)

1. What are you thankful for?

2. Some people have mistakenly thought 1 Thessalonians 5:18 indicates we are to be thankful for the death of a loved one. What does this verse actually say? Explain your answer.

CONSIDER THIS

"I'm grateful I had my father for as long as I did, that he was the person he was, and that God had uniquely given him to me." –Phil Sasser

"I'm so grateful Jesus made it possible for me to see my son again one day." –Hollis

"I am so grateful for our church and how well they've cared for us." –Carla

"I'm thankful I have God on my team because I don't know how I would have survived without Him."
–Phoebe

"I'm thankful God has given me an opportunity to [lead a GriefShare group]." –Jeffery

"I'm grateful to have my family." –Shay

TALKING TO GOD

God, to experience Your peace, You have asked me to bring my fears, anxieties, and requests to You with thanksgiving. This is what I am thankful to You for ...

"I'm thankful we have good people in our life." –Ami

DAY 5

Where will I find the strength?

You're not out there alone. You can endure whatever today might bring. Read the promises in today's Bible passage out loud. They are for you.

GOD'S MESSAGE TO YOU

"God arms me with strength, and he makes my way perfect. He makes me as surefooted as a deer, enabling me to stand on mountain heights. He trains my hands for battle; he strengthens my arm to draw a bronze bow. You have given me your shield of victory. Your right hand supports me; your help has made me great. You have made a wide path for my feet to keep them from slipping." (Psalm 18:32–36 NLT)

1. You are walking on your own path of grief. How would you describe the path under your feet?

2. What did the author of this Psalm believe that God was doing/had done for him?

3. Which part of today's Bible passage do you find most encouraging?

CONSIDER THIS

"When I was grieving Rick's death, I did something really difficult that I didn't want to do ... I reread all the letters he wrote to me when he was in the Army, and just bawled. But after, it was like, 'With God's help, I did it!'" –Dr. Susan Zonnebelt-Smeenge

TALKING TO GOD

God, strengthen me, support me, and keep my feet from slipping as I step out and start doing my grief work.

BRYAN: LOOKING BACK

"God has been able to use the situation to inspire me to do things I otherwise would have never done. Through that, God's been able to show me a purpose, a hope, and a joy that I never asked for, but that I couldn't live without at this point in my life. That gets back to letting go of the things that I thought were important [before Austin died] and letting God direct me to those things that are important."

NEXT SESSION

Learn practical strategies that will help keep you on the path of healing.

"God is alive, and God is going with us into the future." –Carla

MY WEEKLY GRIEF WORK
Session - Nine

PERSONAL CHECKUP – TRACK YOUR HEALING PROGRESS
Place a check in the box identifying how you're feeling. Insert words to explain why.

	REALLY BAD	OKAY	PRETTY GOOD	GREAT
EMOTIONALLY				
PHYSICALLY				
SPIRITUALLY				
RELATIONALLY				

JOURNAL TOPICS – MAKING SENSE OF IT ALL
Choose one or more ideas below, or choose your own topic. We encourage you
to use a separate notebook for your weekly journaling.

Describe ways you've been avoiding your grief and pain.

Worship God in your journal. Thank Him for the relationship you had with your loved one.

Describe how your feelings have been driving your actions and keeping you from doing your grief work.

MOVING FORWARD – PRACTICAL STEPS TOWARD HEALING
HOW TO WORK THROUGH YOUR MISCONCEPTIONS
The wrong beliefs below have caused people to become stuck in grief.
Explain why each of these beliefs are untrue:

Time heals all wounds –

The lessening of pain indicates a lessening of love –

Holding tightly to my grief honors my loved one –

God took something from me that I can't live without –

Progress means taking steps forward, but never steps back –

LESSONS OF GRIEF - PART ONE

YOU NEED HELP TO FACE THE DAYS AHEAD, to take steps forward, to do your grief work, and to remain steady as you go. This session introduces several practical lessons that will help.

Viewing the video and completing your **FROM MOURNING TO JOY** and **MY WEEKLY GRIEF WORK** exercises will help you become more aware of:

  An often-overlooked reason that grief is so painful

  Why going to church can be so difficult

  The benefits of helping others

VIDEO OUTLINE

Use this outline to write down important concepts, encouraging words, or questions you have while viewing the video.

BASIC LESSONS OF GRIEF

You lost more than a person

Firsts and holidays

Plan for difficult days

"The harder I know a day is going to be, the sooner I need to turn to God." –Brad Hambrick

Church may be tough

Pray

Read the Bible   (Psalm 119:50, Philippians 4:13, Psalm 147:3)

Read the Bible

Visualize Scripture   (Psalm 18:29, Deuteronomy 33:12)

Use a checklist

Help others   (2 Corinthians 1:3–4)

"It's a great benefit to be in fellowship ... to be in church." –Phil Sasser

Help Others

Point people to God

You have something to offer

It's a blessing

In this week's From Mourning to Joy exercises ...
After the death of Sharon's son, she struggled with great guilt, anger, and grief, and she discovered the path to peace. Find ways that you can move forward in peace, too.

COPING WITH GRIEF DURING THE HOLIDAY SEASON

In this week's video, you heard about how to handle difficult days, such as anniversaries, birthdays, and other holidays. Holidays such as Thanksgiving and Christmas can introduce an entire season of difficult days. The suggestions in this article can help you face the many traditions, gatherings, and expectations associated with the holiday season.

Prioritizing and planning: Start by making a list of what you would like to accomplish, do, or not do during the holidays; this could include traditions, get-togethers, events, decorations, meals—anything you've done in past years. Then, sit down with your family and allow each person to discuss what his or her preferences and desires would be, too. Encourage each person to be specific about what would be helpful to him or her, and share what would be helpful to you. Allow everyone plenty of leeway as each one will be dealing with different emotions. Be creative; give yourself and your family members permission to do something out of the ordinary when it comes to family celebrations or traditions. Regarding holiday tasks and responsibilities that you usually take care of, ask yourself, "Is this something someone else can do?" (This planning activity can also include extended family and friends.)

Accept your limitations: Grief consumes your energy no matter what the season. Holidays place additional demands on time and emotions. Expect fluctuations in your mood and perspective. Lower your expectations to accommodate your current needs. Flexibility is the key word during this time. Your needs will change, so keep family and friends aware of what you're thinking and feeling. For instance, if you are invited to a get-together, you might choose to say yes, but also give the hostess a forewarning that you might end up not coming at the last minute or having to leave early.

Accommodate changes that came with your circumstances, and find ways to decrease your stress: Consider changing your surroundings or your traditions to decrease your stress. Be honest with family and friends and let them know things might be different this year. Limit social, family, and church commitments to your existing energy level. Another suggestion is to shop early, use catalogs, or shop online. Look at the priorities you've listed and reevaluate them. Leave out unnecessary activities or obligations that you've either placed on yourself or that others may want to place on you.

Ask for and accept help: Accept offers of assistance with holidays—shopping, decorating, cleaning, cooking, etc. Your loved ones and friends might be looking for ways to come alongside you and lessen your pain. Allow them to support you in concrete ways. Let them do or help with the thing you would like to see done, yet have no energy to do. Bottom line, there is no "formula" for dealing with grief or loss over the holidays that will make everything better. You are walking in an unknown territory, but God promises His children that He will never leave nor forsake us (Hebrews 13:5b). Learn all you can from what you are called upon to endure so that in time you can come alongside someone else and comfort that person with the comfort you were given (2 Corinthians 1:3-4).

To learn more about the topics shared in this article, take time to read the following Scriptures: **Faith:** Hebrews 11:1, Colossians 1:23; **Comfort:** 2 Corinthians 1:3-4; **Courage:** Isaiah 41:10; **Remembering:** Philippians 1:3, Psalm 111:4; **Love:** Romans 8:37-39; **Hope:** Psalm 71:14, Romans 5:1-5.

For helpful articles and videos on how to survive the holiday season, and to find a *GriefShare Surviving the Holidays* seminar near you, go to www.griefshare.org/holidays.

SHARON: "I HAD BEEN FIGHTING WITH THE LORD"

Sharon experienced the death of her young son, who had drowned. "I felt like I had been fighting with the Lord. There was warfare in my soul between Satan telling me to hold on to my grief and bitterness, and God telling me to let it go. I went to my son's bedroom, and I cried and pleaded with the Lord. But I needed peace, and I knew I had to submit to the Lord for peace to happen ..."

You can receive peace and comfort for your journey, too. This week's exercises discuss important lessons to learn and apply on how to move through grief.

DAY 1

Internalizing Scripture
Reading God's Word, taking it in and consuming it, brings great comfort and healing.

GOD'S MESSAGE TO YOU
"The instructions of the LORD are perfect, reviving the soul ... The commandments of the LORD are right, bringing joy to the heart. The commands of the LORD are clear, giving insight for living." (Psalm 19:7–8 NLT)

1. What are some benefits of internalizing God's Word, according to Psalm 19:7–8?

2. What three words are used to describe God's instructions/commands in Psalm 19:7–8?

3. Write down ideas of ways you can start getting into God's Word more. (See today's "Consider this" section for more ideas.)

CONSIDER THIS

"We had some CDs with songs that were all Scripture, and I would sit sometimes for hours and close my eyes and [listen] because I was too weary to read the Bible. I would feel like my cup was being refilled." –Ann

"Reading through the Psalms was a tremendous help." –Sharon

Meet with a mature Christian believer who can help you understand scriptural truths. Attend a Bible study.

Take a "guided tour" of Bible topics by using an on-line reading plan. You can find easy-to-follow Bible reading plans at ***www.bible.com/reading-plans***.

"Church is where God is the focus, eternal life is spoken of, and comfort is given." –Phil Sasser

Write Bible truths on paper or electronic devices so you can read them throughout your day. Place a verse on your screensaver. Change your ringtones to uplifting Christian music.

TALKING TO GOD

God, Your Word is living and active. It is able to reach the deepest aches in our heart and provide comfort and healing.

Visualizing Scripture
DAY 2
Today's exercise will be done in your head, so you do not need a pen!

On the videos, Joyce Rogers explains how visualizing Scripture can help make your Bible reading more real and personal. It involves reading a Bible passage, slowly picturing the details in your mind, and picturing how you personally fit into the picture.

GOD'S MESSAGE TO YOU
"Even though the fig trees have no blossoms, and there are no grapes on the vines; even though the olive crop fails, and the fields lie empty and barren; even though the flocks die in the fields, and the cattle barns are empty, yet I will rejoice in the LORD! I will be joyful in the God of my salvation! The Sovereign LORD is my strength! He makes me as surefooted as a deer, able to tread upon the heights." (Habakkuk 3:17–19 NLT)

1. Read these six steps first, and then apply them to today's Bible passage. You will be picturing each portion of Habakkuk 3:17–19 step by step. Spend time visualizing slowly and in great detail all the words.

2. Place yourself right in the middle of this picture.

3. Picture your responses to the scene as you read.

4. Visualize how, by faith, you turn to God in this scene.

5. Picture how God strengthens and helps you.

6. Picture how this can be applied to your personal situation.

TALKING TO GOD

Thank you, God for the promise that You will be my strength as I walk on this difficult, desolate path. Thank you that You can give me joy alongside my sorrow.

Going to church is hard
DAY 3
"I didn't go to church for months." –Stephen

GOD'S MESSAGE TO YOU
"Not giving up meeting together, as some are in the habit of doing, but encouraging one another–and all the more as you see the Day approaching." (Hebrews 10:25)

1. Describe any struggles you have with going to church now.

2. What does Hebrews 10:25 say about going to church?

3. What are some practical ideas you can do to help make it a little easier to be in church?

Ideas to help you ease back into church:

- Arrive late and/or leave early.

- Sit in the back row.

- Sit with someone who will run interference for you and help you interact with people.

- Identify a place ahead of time where you can go if you're emotionally overwhelmed.

- Attend with someone who will understand when you're ready to leave.

- Let your pastor know you are there, so he can be aware of ways he might be able to help you.

"I realized I needed church, because it gives me strength; it is positive; it's encouraging. It's everything I need to get through life and to get through this grief."
–Shay

TALKING TO GOD

God, I know that part of my healing is to spend time with other people in a church setting, focusing on and worshipping You. Give me the strength to do this.

DAY 4

Helping others helps you
Don't wait until you feel better to begin helping others.

"Sometimes the best remedy for grief is finding some way to touch somebody else's life." –Dr. Larry Crabb

GOD'S MESSAGE TO YOU
"Serve one another humbly in love." (Galatians 5:13b)

1. People all around us are facing stresses, hardships, and losses. Why do you think you're better qualified now to help someone who is struggling?

2. When we reach out and help another person, what should our heart attitude be, according to Galatians 5:13b?

3. Prayerfully ask God whom you could help. Write down ideas of different ways you could reach out and help people. (It could be a simple, one-time act of kindness, or it could be a regular service.)

CONSIDER THIS

"My sister-in-law has three preschoolers, and I would go over and weed her flower beds. I was reaching out to somebody. I was physically active. Those two things brought a lot of healing for me." –Sharon

TALKING TO GOD

God, with Your enabling, I have something to offer people, even in the midst of my pain. Show me who needs my help, my care, and my energy.

DAY 5

Praying
Prayer is talking with God. You can talk to God anytime, any place. You don't have to use formal words or special phrases. And God understands that sometimes we feel we don't have any words to pray at all.

GOD'S MESSAGE TO YOU
"Is anyone among you in trouble? Let them pray." (James 5:13a)

"I found that as I served someone else, it lessened my pain." –Nancy Guthrie

"In the same way, the Spirit helps us in our weakness. We do not know what we ought to pray for, but the Spirit himself intercedes for us through wordless groans." (Romans 8:26)

1. What do you think might happen if you spent more time praying about your situation?

2. According to Romans 8:26, if you are a Christian, how does God help you when you have no words to pray?*

* To learn more about how to ensure you are a Christian, read "God, What Is Going On?" on page xii.

3. Write a prayer to God below, telling Him anything that's weighing on your mind and asking for His guidance.

CONSIDER THIS

"When I feel anxious, when I feel tempted, when I feel nervous, when I feel out of control, when I feel worried, I take that to [God, who is seated on] the throne of Grace, with great intentionality, and I tie it to the altar. I thank Him ahead of time for the outcome."
—Dr. Crawford Loritts

TALKING TO GOD

God, help me to make prayer a part of my daily life, a moment-by-moment experience with You.

SHARON: LOOKING BACK

"Instead of saying, 'Why did You take my child? Why did You let this happen to me?' I'm saying, 'Okay Lord, You brought me to this point in my life. What do You have for me to do next?' I was willing at that point to let God work through me to help others, and that's when the total healing process started–when I was able to let go of my anger, my guilt, and my self-will and to say, 'God take control. I'm willing to let You work good through this tragedy.'"

NEXT SESSION
Discover what your grief is teaching you.

"The Spirit of God empowers us to do the impossible." –Dr. Crawford Loritts

MY WEEKLY GRIEF WORK

Session - Ten

PERSONAL CHECKUP – TRACK YOUR HEALING PROGRESS
Place a check in the box identifying how you're feeling. Insert words to explain why.

	REALLY BAD	OKAY	PRETTY GOOD	GREAT
EMOTIONALLY				
PHYSICALLY				
SPIRITUALLY				
RELATIONALLY				

JOURNAL TOPICS – MAKING SENSE OF IT ALL
Choose one or more ideas below, or choose your own topic. We encourage you
to use a separate notebook for your weekly journaling.

- Write down your fears and anxieties about going to church. Then write steps you will take to ease back into church. (See Day 3, page 100, for ideas.)

- Before the death of your loved one, you claimed to believe (and not believe) certain things. How have your beliefs changed or been tested?

MOVING FORWARD – PRACTICAL STEPS TOWARD HEALING
HOW TO IDENTIFY AND GRIEVE SECONDARY LOSSES
You have lost more than a person: you've also lost everything that person was to you. Today you'll begin the necessary step of identifying and grieving your multiple losses. We suggest you write these in your journal or on a separate page.

1. Write down what you've lost in that person (categories and examples to the right are given as a guide; you'll want to develop your own list).

2. Say your losses out loud to God and grieve each loss separately, asking for God's comfort and guidance.

3. Come back to this exercise as the weeks go on and add to the list.

Chores/Responsibilities
– my cook, my mechanic, the bill-payer

Child care/Nurturing
– the one who reads to the kids, makes them laugh

Hopes and dreams
– retiring together, future milestones

On a personal note
– my companion, my snuggler

LESSONS OF
GRIEF - PART TWO

IF YOU PERSEVERE, YOUR GRIEF can teach you invaluable lessons. You might not want to learn them. But others who've completed the journey of grief say these lessons, while painful, are worth learning.

This week, the three aspects of GriefShare—video, discussion, and workbook exercises—combine together to bring you a more complete picture of:

 Who you are now that your loved one is gone

 Why no one grieves perfectly

Ⓘ What grief can teach you about relationships

VIDEO OUTLINE

Use this outline to write down important concepts, encouraging words, or questions you have while viewing the video.

DIFFICULT LESSONS

Grief is not an identity

Grief Is Not an Identity

Who are you?

Resisting a new identity

More like Christ   (Romans 8:28–29, Luke 22:42)

"This experience doesn't define me. Christ defines me." –Dr. Paul David Tripp

The value of relationships

Depend more on God

James: "Learn to embrace it"   (2 Corinthians 4:8–9)

No one grieves perfectly

No One Grieves Perfectly

Susan: "I was wrong"

God loves & forgives   (Psalm 32)

Preparation for future trials   (Philippians 1:6)

In this week's From Mourning to Joy exercises ...

JoAnne shares how she moved from not knowing who she was anymore to becoming more comfortable in her new identity. Read this week's exercises to continue moving forward on your own grief journey.

"Life is really about loving God and loving others." –Carla

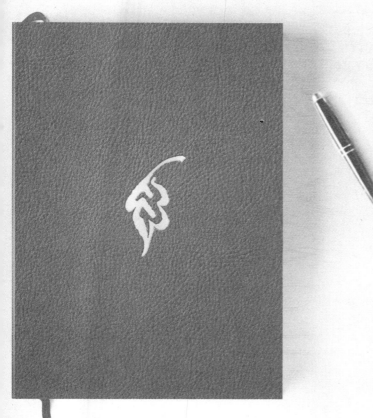

JOANNE: "I DIDN'T KNOW WHO I WAS"

"I had defined myself like someone who was needed for so long: as a wife, a mother. And then as Jody [my husband] was dying, I was there to strengthen, encourage, and comfort him—and now that was all gone. It was like I didn't even know who I was anymore."

Grief can leave you floundering, so much so that you don't even know who you are anymore. If you begin to focus on grief as your identity, you'll fail to look up, look around, and see what you can learn from your situation. This week's exercises discuss some important lessons of grief. Please read each one and prayerfully allow God to work in your heart as you consider His truths.

Grief is not an identity

DAY 1

These are the thoughts of someone who has taken on grief as an identity:

Don't expect me to enjoy myself ... I'm still grieving.

I'm not going to help someone else ... I've got my own wounds to care for.

This is my lot in life ... to grieve.

Making plans won't make a difference ... grieving people don't have schedules.

Stop annoying me with your invitations ... you know grieving people don't want to go anywhere.

I'm not going to pursue my own interests ... I'm only going to do what my loved one and I enjoyed.

Please understand, in the early days of grief, your focus is going to be on your grief and its all-consuming nature, and that's okay. But your grief shouldn't become your identity.

GOD'S MESSAGE TO YOU
"So in Christ Jesus you are all children of God through faith ... There is neither Jew nor Gentile, neither slave nor free, nor is there male and female, for you are all one in Christ Jesus." (Galatians 3:26, 28)

1. According to today's Bible passage, Christians are those who, through faith, are what?*

* Read the article on page xii to find out what it means to be a Christian.

2. This passage tells us that significant aspects of a person's identity (race, status, gender) are not as important as his position in Christ. What does this imply about how God primarily wants you to see yourself?

3. How will you define yourself? Write your answer in the form of a prayer to God.

"If I'm defined by the way God sees me, that gives me hope." –Dr. Larry Crabb

"My primary identity is, I'm loved by my Savior. That is where I have to find everything I am."
–Elyse Fitzpatrick

"See what great love the Father has lavished on us, that we should be called children of God! And that is what we are!" –1 John 3:1a

TALKING TO GOD

God, I am loved by You. I am Your child. I can rely on Your strength and Your promises. I have a purpose in You.

 DAY 2

God uses suffering to help us grow

Grief teaches us valuable lessons about our relationships with others and our relationship with God.

GOD'S MESSAGE TO YOU

"Consider it pure joy, my brothers and sisters, whenever you face trials of many kinds, because you know that the testing of your faith produces perseverance. Let perseverance finish its work so that you may be mature and complete, not lacking anything." (James 1:2–4)

1. James 1:2–4 does not mean to be happy about what happened. Instead, what reasons does this passage give for being joyful in the midst of trials?

2. What lessons has grief taught you?

About persevering in your faith:

About your relationships:

CONSIDER THIS

JoAnne shares some of the lessons she has learned in her grief:

- *Relationships are so important to me. I work harder to keep them healthy.*
- *I learned that God means what He says.*
- *I discovered I could really encourage people who are hurting.*

TALKING TO GOD

God, give me the grace to persevere. This grief can make me bitter for the rest of my life, or it can make me better. Help me to accept this suffering and to be open to learn from it.

 DAY 3

God always turns bad to good

Certain things in your life look pretty bad right now. The most amazing hope you can receive into your life comes with the promise that God always overcomes suffering and evil with good.

GOD'S MESSAGE TO YOU

Joseph's brothers betrayed and abandoned him. He was forced to live far from home, facing slavery, prison, and false accusations. Eventually, through a series of events only God could have orchestrated, Joseph became the highest official in the Egyptian palace under Pharaoh and was able to help many people survive a famine. Years later, Joseph faced his brothers again.

"But Joseph said to them, '…You intended to harm me, but God intended it for good to accomplish what is now being done, the saving of many lives. So then, don't be afraid. I will provide for you and your children.' And he reassured them and spoke kindly to them." (Genesis 50:19–21)

"The cross is the ultimate argument for God using bad for good." –Dr. Paul David Tripp

1. Joseph was in a powerful position to do or say anything he wanted to his brothers, whom he was seeing for the first time after their hateful deed. Describe Joseph's response to the situation.

2. What good things did God accomplish through a very bad situation (see Genesis 50:19–21)?

3. Why do you think God wants you to know that He always brings good out of what is bad?

CONSIDER THIS

God always overcomes evil with good. He can take the bad things that happen, the bad decisions of people and the terrible consequences of those decisions, and turn them around to bring about good.

TALKING TO GOD

God, it doesn't feel right to even consider that good might come out of my loved one's death. But, this is where I think I know what's going on, when really I don't. Help me understand that there is a bigger picture. You know what You're doing.

DAY 4

God is good
God is good, and He proved it when Jesus died on the cross.

GOD'S MESSAGE TO YOU
"Very rarely will anyone die for a righteous person ... But God demonstrates his own love for us in this: While we were still sinners, Christ died for us. Since we have now been justified by his blood, how much more shall we be saved from God's wrath through him!" (Romans 5:7–9)

1. How does Romans 5:7–9 say God has demonstrated His love for us?

2. In what kind of spiritual condition were we in when Christ died for us (see Romans 5:7–9)?

3. Other Bible passages (Ephesians 2:1–3 and Romans 3:10–11) make it clear that, as sinners, we wanted nothing to do with God, yet God still gave His Son for us. What does that tell you about God's character?

CONSIDER THIS

"When bad things happen, I start wondering, 'God, are you really good?' That's where the cross comes in: how can you argue that God isn't good if He did that? If He sent His Son to die for me, then I've got to say that He really is good." –Dr. Larry Crabb

"[Be] intentional about reminding yourself of God's goodness and looking at the bigger picture." –Lois Rabey

TALKING TO GOD

Jesus, Your death on the cross was the worst evil, and You overcame it with a greater good. You came so that we could have life. When I confess my sins to You and believe in the goodness of Your sacrifice, my grief won't disappear, but I'll be able to move forward because I can see a bigger picture now of what goodness means.

DAY 5

Repentance is part of your grief process
That moment when you realize even your grief is tainted by sin ...

"In my grief I lashed out at a lot of people." –Jodi

"I cling to that truth that I know God loves me because He sent His Son for me." –John

"I had anger. I had jealousy. I had self-pity issues."
—JoAnne

"I chose to blame [my aunt and uncle] ... I pushed them away for eight years." —Iris

"I distrusted [God], didn't like Him, and was trying to use His own words against Him." —Susan Lutz

GOD'S MESSAGE TO YOU

"If we claim to be without sin, we deceive ourselves and the truth is not in us. If we confess our sins, he is faithful and just and will forgive us our sins and purify us from all unrighteousness." (1 John 1:8–9)

"Search me, God, and know my heart; test me and know my anxious thoughts. See if there is any offensive way in me, and lead me in the way everlasting." (Psalm 139:23–24)

1. In what ways have you used your grief as an excuse for mistreating other people?

2. According to 1 John 1:8–9, what should we do once we realize we've done something wrong? What is the result?

3. Read Psalm 139:23–24 as your prayer right now. Write down anything that comes to mind that you need to repent of.

CONSIDER THIS

"Anytime God shows you something that's amiss in your life, it's not to push you away, it's to pull you closer." —Susan Lutz

Repentance involves turning from your sin and doing something else in its place. It's not a one-time thing. We do it over and over in life and will have to do it multiple times as we grieve.

TALKING TO GOD

God, I agree that what You've revealed to me about my behaviors is wrong. I want to make a sincere effort to turn from this sin and handle it differently next time. Thank you for Your love, mercy, and patience with me, and for Your forgiveness.

JOANNE: LOOKING BACK

"I started to see myself as a single woman who was sad, but was making it. I was lonely, but I was dealing with it, because God was helping me and He was making me into a different person. At first I thought God took what I needed away from me, but He didn't. He gave me more of Himself, and that's all any of us need. God was becoming a reality in my life more and more, and it was really a learning process. As I was seeing how God would help me, then I was trusting Him more. It was building my confidence. As that grew, I was starting to feel more comfortable with my new identity: my new identity as a single person who had to trust God and get His guidance in making good decisions."

NEXT SESSION
Get a glimpse of what you can look forward to in heaven.

"God stands ready to forgive us, and He treats us with grace and patience, even as we grow." —Dr. Stephen Viars

MY WEEKLY GRIEF WORK

Session - Eleven

PERSONAL CHECKUP – TRACK YOUR HEALING PROGRESS

Place a check in the box identifying how you're feeling. Insert words to explain why.

	REALLY BAD	OKAY	PRETTY GOOD	GREAT
EMOTIONALLY				
PHYSICALLY				
SPIRITUALLY				
RELATIONALLY				

JOURNAL TOPICS – MAKING SENSE OF IT ALL

Choose one or more ideas below, or choose your own topic. We encourage you
to use a separate notebook for your weekly journaling.

✒ What are the most significant lessons you are learning through your grief?

✒ Dr. Joseph Stowell says, "Self-sufficiency is a terrible place to be because it is the worst deceit we can bring on ourselves. We need God." Explain how this is true for you.

✒ When you look at the cross—the cross where Jesus was crucified to take on the punishment for our sins so that we might live forever with Him—you will see that out of horrific evil came the ultimate good. Have you had an experience of something good coming out of something bad? Write about this experience.

MOVING FORWARD – PRACTICAL STEPS TOWARD HEALING
HOW TO FIGURE OUT YOUR NEW IDENTITY

On the video, H. Norman Wright shares this suggestion.

1. In your own handwriting, write a title on the blank line below: "Who I Am Now."

2. Using as many descriptive words as possible, write down who you are in the following categories. (Use a separate paper as needed.)

Title: _____

Relationally –

Emotionally –

Career/Work, including volunteer and service –

Skills/Interests/Hobbies/Passions –

Spiritually, in God's eyes –

HEAVEN

SINCE YOUR LOVED ONE'S DEATH, you've probably starting thinking more about heaven, what it's like, and what happens when a person dies. Knowing the truth about heaven is a source of great hope.

Today's session will answer many questions about heaven and the afterlife. For example:

 What is heaven like?

 Should I communicate with my deceased loved one?

Are near-death experiences reliable descriptions of heaven?

And many more ...

VIDEO OUTLINE

Use this outline to write down important concepts, encouraging words, or questions you have while viewing the video.

THE JOYS OF HEAVEN

Reunited   (1 Corinthians 2:9)

It's wonderful   (Matthew 6:9–10, Revelation 21:3–5)

Heaven described

"We can endure the pain of this life because of the promise of life to come." –Hank Hanegraaff

We'll see Jesus   (2 Samuel 12:23)

Death will die   (Revelation 7)

QUESTIONS ABOUT THE AFTERLIFE

Heavenly bodies?   (2 Corinthians 5:8)

Cremation?

Talking to the dead?   (Deuteronomy 18:10b–12a)

Near-death experiences?

Reincarnation?

What if my loved one isn't in heaven?   (2 Peter 3:9)

"Your heart will never be the same, but it won't always be broken." –Dr. Joseph Stowell

Do all religions lead to heaven?   (John 14:6, Psalm 5:4)

In this week's From Mourning to Joy exercises ...
Cindy experienced a miracle moment from God, giving her hope and reassurance during a tough time. In this week's daily exercises, you'll find hope when you learn God's promises about heaven, eternal life, and being reunited with loved ones.

GOD'S FORGIVENESS: AN UNLIKELY SOURCE OF JOY AND COMFORT

In the midst of grief we turn to many things for comfort–food, friends, memorabilia, time alone. But we often overlook a source of joy and comfort: God's forgiveness.

Admitting your shortcomings and experiencing God's forgiveness spares you from an eternity of suffering and separation from God. That's why the Bible says forgiveness is a source of joy:

"But I trust in your unfailing love. I will rejoice because you have rescued me." (Psalm 13:5 NLT)

HOW TO EXPERIENCE GOD'S FORGIVENESS

If you've never experienced God's forgiveness, we encourage you to pray the following prayer from your heart. If you do, your grief won't instantly lift, but you'll always have an unshakable source of comfort to lean on as you work through your grief.

Dear God, I know I've done things that offend You. Thank you so much for sending Jesus to suffer and die on the cross in my place. Thank you for giving me a perfect standing in Your sight through His death. Please lead me and guide me. You're in charge. Show me what I should do in every area of my life. Amen.

THE JOYS OF FORGIVENESS

When things get tough, and they will, reflect on these truths about your forgiveness:

- God has no anger toward me for anything I've done wrong. He poured out His anger over my sin on Christ, who suffered and died for my sin, in my place. (1 John 2:2)

- God loves me enough that He sacrificed His own Son to meet my deepest need. This proves His love for me. (Romans 5:8)

- God has spared me from unimaginable suffering and qualified me to experience eternal paradise. (Colossians 1:12–14)

HOW TO COMFORT YOURSELF

Meditating on these truths won't change your immediate circumstances, but these truths can be a source of joy, happiness, and hope in the midst of your grief. Consider memorizing some of the Bible verses that support these truths so you can reflect on them anytime. Ask God to make you more and more aware of how much you are in need of His forgiveness and grace.

"Christ died the death I should have died. That is the comfort of all comforts." –Phil Sasser

"Blessed [happy] is the one whose transgressions are forgiven, whose sins are covered. Blessed [happy] is the one whose sin the LORD does not count against them and in whose spirit is no deceit." (Psalm 32:1–2)

CINDY: "I WILL SEE YOU SOON"

"Earlier that day, David [my fiancé] had left a phone message on my voicemail, and it said, 'Hey beautiful. Just checking in to see how this day is going. I know this is going to be a long, hard day. I'm not going to call and bug you, because I know you've got a lot going on. But just know, Cindy, I love you. I am proud of you. And I will see you soon.' That was about 8 o'clock in the morning when he had left that message ...'"

God wants us to know that a person's death is not the end for that person. In this week's **From Mourning to Joy**, you'll receive a taste of what God has promised regarding life after death and heaven.

DAY 1 — No more tears, suffering, or death

Our lives and our loved one's lives are chapters in the middle of a much larger story. And the conclusion of that story, God says, is awesome!

GOD'S MESSAGE TO YOU

"He will wipe every tear from their eyes. There will be no more death or mourning or crying or pain, for the old order of things has passed away. He who was seated on the throne said, 'I am making everything new!'" (Revelation 21:4–5a)

"May the God of hope fill you with all joy and peace as you trust in him, so that you may overflow with hope by the power of the Holy Spirit." (Romans 15:13)

1. What have you felt hopeless about?

2. What does Revelation 21:4–5a say is the conclusion of life's story (for people who have believed in Christ)?

3. What are the benefits of trusting God with your situation (see Romans 15:13)?

CONSIDER THIS

"There's a big difference between thinking about 'This is a bad chapter' and 'This is the last chapter.'"
–Dr. Stephen Viars

Because of what Christ has done for you, you can grieve with hope.

TALKING TO GOD

God, I'm glad this isn't the final chapter of my life or my loved one's life. Help me to take steps to learn more about what You've promised for this life and the next.

DAY 2

We'll see our loved ones again

"I know my daughter is in heaven and she's safe. I know I'm going to see my child again. The Bible promises me that." –Ann

GOD'S MESSAGE TO YOU

"And now, dear brothers and sisters, we want you to know what will happen to the believers who have died so you will not grieve like people who have no hope. For since we believe that Jesus died and was raised to life again, we also believe that when Jesus returns, God will bring back with him the believers who have died." (1 Thessalonians 4:13–14 NLT)

1. God says if you are a believer in Christ, you are to grieve differently than everyone else. Why? What is the difference (see 1 Thessalonians 4:13–14)?

2. According to 1 Thessalonians 4:13–14, what do Christians believe?

3. How might this verse help someone who believes Christians shouldn't be sorrowful over the death of a loved one?

CONSIDER THIS

"And if our hope in Christ is only for this life, we are more to be pitied than anyone in the world. But in fact, Christ has been raised from the dead. He is the first of a great harvest of all who have died ... everyone who belongs to Christ will be given new life."
–1 Corinthians 15:19–22 NLT

TALKING TO GOD

God, I want to grieve like one who has hope: not an "I hope so" hope, but true, biblical assurance that this will come to pass.

DAY 3

How does anyone get into heaven?

If God doesn't allow sin (anything we do that displeases Him) to reside in His presence, doesn't that disqualify all of us from getting into heaven?

GOD'S MESSAGE TO YOU

"For you are not a God who is pleased with wickedness; with you, evil people [people who have done wrong] are not welcome." (Psalm 5:4)

"Your eyes are too pure to look on evil; you cannot tolerate wrongdoing." (Habakkuk 1:13a)

"And we have believed in Christ Jesus, so that we might be made right with God because of our faith in Christ." (Galatians 2:16b NLT)

1. According to Psalm 5:4, what kind of people are not welcome in heaven?

2. Why does God not allow sin to live in His presence (see Habakkuk 1:13a)?

"We sorrow, but not like those who don't have hope." –Dr. Stephen Viars

3. If God won't allow sinful people to reside in His presence, on what grounds do you think God will let you into heaven (see Galatians 2:16b)?

CONSIDER THIS

No one will be granted access to heaven on his own merit, but ...

"God made Christ, who never sinned, to be the offering for our sin, so that we could be made right with God through Christ." –2 Corinthians 5:21 NLT

"When God saves us, He makes us new, instantly. When He looks at us, we are a hundred percent okay. We have Christ's righteousness." –Susan Lutz

TALKING TO GOD

God, in Jesus I can be freed from sin and live eternally in Your presence! Thank you! I know that I've done things that offend You. Thank you for sending Jesus to suffer and die on the cross in my place, to be condemned for my sake. Thank you for giving me a perfect standing in Your sight. Please lead me and guide me. You're in charge. Show me what I should do in every area of my life.

The only path to heaven

DAY 4

Some people claim that all religions lead to heaven. Others say that everyone who is basically good, honest, and hardworking goes to heaven. What does God say?

GOD'S MESSAGE TO YOU
"Jesus answered, 'I am the way and the truth and the life. No one comes to the Father except through me.'" (John 14:6)

"Salvation is found in no one else, for there is no other name under heaven given to mankind by which we must be saved." (Acts 4:12)

1. What have you believed in the past about who goes to heaven?

2. What does God say, according to John 14:6 and Acts 4:12?

3. How certain are you of your eternal destiny?*

* If you are not certain, read the article on page xii to learn more about how to place your faith in Jesus and secure your place in heaven.

CONSIDER THIS

Heaven is a wonderful place. But the only way to spend eternity with God there is to believe in Jesus Christ. Please take time to consider this important topic. Your eternal destiny depends on it.

"If you declare with your mouth, 'Jesus is Lord,' and believe in your heart that God raised him from the dead, you will be saved ... for, 'Everyone who calls on the name of the Lord will be saved.'" –Romans 10:9, 13

TALKING TO GOD

God, I realize that getting into heaven is a choice, and it's not a choice of "where" I'm going, it's "Whom" I'm surrendering my life to. Jesus, I know I'm a sinner and that I need You desperately. I believe You died on the cross to pay my sin-debt to God and to enable me to live now and eternally in freedom and rest.

IS MY LOVED ONE IN HEAVEN?

If you're concerned your loved one isn't in heaven, keep in mind that your loved one may have become a Christian without you knowing it. Simply coming to God in faith, believing Christ died on the

"Our loved ones who died in Christ are in a place of total fulfillment." –Phil Sasser

cross for you, saves you from sin. In some cases, you don't know for sure what your loved one believed or whether your loved one's beliefs changed prior to the death.

The wonders of heaven

DAY 5

Heaven is far better than anything you can imagine on earth. The best thing about heaven is that Jesus Christ will be there. It may be hard for you to imagine how glorious and wonderful that will be. You will be completely satisfied to the deepest levels of your soul in heaven with Jesus Christ.

GOD'S MESSAGE TO YOU

"Come, you who are blessed by my Father; take your inheritance, the kingdom prepared for you since the creation of the world." (Matthew 25:34b)

1. If you have given God control of your life, you are now His child, His heir. What is the inheritance that He promises you?

2. Describe a moment in your life that brought you great joy.

3. Describe a time when you saw something extraordinarily beautiful.

4. Name some people whom you love dearly.

5. Consider these wonderful moments and people, and be assured that the glories of heaven are multiplied far beyond all these put together. Take a moment to thank God.

CONSIDER THIS

"Make no mistake about it: the thing that makes heaven heaven is the fact that God is there."
–Anne Graham Lotz

"I am the Alpha and the Omega–the Beginning and the End. To all who are thirsty I will give freely from the springs of the water of life. All who are victorious will inherit all these blessings, and I will be their God, and they will be my children."
–Revelation 21:6b–7 NLT

TALKING TO GOD

Thank you, God, for providing this incredible inheritance for Your children! Please give me the strength to persevere until I get there.

CINDY: LOOKING BACK

"I talked to David at 5:15 p.m. and at 5:30 he was killed. Later that night, I realized I had that message, and I pulled it up from my voicemail at work and listened to it again. It was amazing to hear the words: 'Hey beautiful. I'm not going to call you, but I am proud of you. And I'll see you soon.'"

NEXT SESSION
Discover how to continue moving forward in your grief.

"[In] heaven, our discovery of God is going to be an eternal adventure." –Joni Eareckson Tada

MY WEEKLY GRIEF WORK

Session - Twelve

PERSONAL CHECKUP – TRACK YOUR HEALING PROGRESS
Place a check in the box identifying how you're feeling. Insert words to explain why.

	REALLY BAD	OKAY	PRETTY GOOD	GREAT
EMOTIONALLY				
PHYSICALLY				
SPIRITUALLY				
RELATIONALLY				

JOURNAL TOPICS – MAKING SENSE OF IT ALL
Choose one or more ideas below, or choose your own topic. We encourage you to use a separate notebook for your weekly journaling.

✎ How do thoughts of heaven help you endure daily difficulties?

✎ What have you been taught to believe about the afterlife? Have these beliefs undergone any changes? If yes, how so?

✎ Write about a miracle moment you've experienced.

MOVING FORWARD – PRACTICAL STEPS TOWARD HEALING
HOW TO CHANGE YOUR PERSPECTIVE
Seeing your situation from an eternal perspective is a necessary part of learning to grieve with hope.

1. Read God's Word. Go back and read the Scriptures written out in Session 12's **From Mourning to Joy** (some are found in the "Consider this" sections too).

2. Write down which Scripture meant most to you this week and why.

3. Focus on God's Word. Reread the Scripture, underlining key truths. Meditate on these truths. (See the Session 8 My Weekly Grief Work, page 84, for direction on how to meditate on God's Word.)

4. Apply God's Word. Pray, asking God what truth can be applied to your situation and how you can live it out. Write down a possible application.

MyGriefShare+

Your group is ending but your healing has just begun

Your personal GriefShare video library

$25 annual subscription

Continue healing with GriefShare's new video streaming service

Just because your group is coming to a close doesn't mean your healing has to. Subscribe today to MyGriefShare+ to access a personal library of hundreds of GriefShare videos.

With this annual subscription service, you can:

- Access 200+ videos essential to your healing
- Get more advice from popular GriefShare experts & testimonials
- Find answers to the questions you have about your grief
- Learn more about your grief by watching previous editions of GriefShare

NEW CONTENT ADDED MONTHLY

Subscribe today!

GRIEFSHARE.ORG/PLUS

WHAT DO I LIVE FOR NOW?

"WHAT'S NEXT? WHERE DO I GO FROM HERE? How do I get there? What if I don't think I'm ready?" In order for your pain to subside, you have to reengage in life and move forward. This week we'll offer advice for moving forward in your grief in a way that honors your loved one and God.

The video, discussion time, and workbook exercises are filled with advice on how to continue moving forward. You'll learn:

- Why moving forward is a necessity

- Why it's a process

- Why peace and pain will always coexist

VIDEO OUTLINE

Use this outline to write down important concepts, encouraging words, or questions you have while viewing the video.

MOVING FORWARD (5th goal of your grief journey)

A necessity

It's a process

Dealing with stress & anxiety (Matthew 6:34)

"If I only ever look in the rearview mirror, I'm not going to be able to go forward." –Sandy Elder

Ask for help

Know what you need   (Galatians 6:2)

Visiting a counselor

Store memories (6th goal of your grief journey)

Using stored memories

Remember & continue the legacy

A reason for hope

Peace & pain coexist   (John 16:33)

"If you don't know your purpose, this is a great opportunity to begin to discover it." –Sabrina D. Black

In this week's From Mourning to Joy exercises ...
You'll learn keys to moving forward in a way that's healthy, while still cherishing your loved one's memory and legacy.

Reflections

A GRIEF JOURNAL BY GRIEFSHARE

A deeper look at this powerful tool

Discover more about the *Reflections* journal and see how it can help you continue healing after your GriefShare experience ends.

A guided journal

You've heard the benefits of journaling, but simply putting raw emotions on paper isn't enough. This journal offers probing questions that guide your writing and reflections, bringing self-discovery, stability, and hope. It features three types of journaling, helpful tips, and ample space for free-form writing.

A beautiful, high-quality book

What goes on in a grieving person's heart is personal and precious. That's why we designed a book that exemplifies the value of your thoughts and cherished memories, and celebrates your growth. Features include premium paper, a ribbon bookmark, beautiful artwork, and a textured hard cover.

A look inside

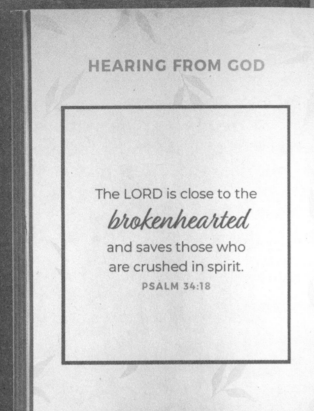

HEARING FROM GOD

> The LORD is close to the *brokenhearted* and saves those who are crushed in spirit.
>
> PSALM 34:18

Reflections

How are you feeling deep down? What has grief done to your heart and spirit?

What do you think about the statement that God is "close to the brokenhearted"?

105

Your journal contains quotes, Scriptures, and questions designed to guide you to deeper levels of healing.

Reflections

The next step on your healing journey

SUSAN: "YOU HAVE TO DO WHAT YOU'RE CALLED TO DO"

"If I were to die tomorrow and Jesus said, 'What have you done with the gifts and the abilities I've given you?' 'Well, I laid on the couch and protected my own being ...'

"He didn't say this was going to be an easy path. He didn't say you aren't going to have to work hard. He said, 'Follow Me,' and you have to do what you're called to do, and He will place you where you're supposed to be."

Moving forward in your grief doesn't mean forgetting your loved one, rather, it involves cherishing and enjoying the precious memories and living out that person's good legacy. Moving forward is not easy, and you'll take steps forward and steps back again. But this week's exercises will give you tools to help.

DAY 1

Handling stress and anxiety

Anxious people want control of their circumstances, thinking that being in control will eliminate their worries. Letting go of anxiety involves trust: trust that God is in control and is working to bring about what is good and best for us.

We want to trust Him, but how do we do it?

Trust is a place of surrender, of laying down what's important to our human nature and embracing God's best instead.

GOD'S MESSAGE TO YOU

"Cursed are those who ... rely on human strength and turn their hearts away from the LORD. They are like stunted shrubs in the desert, with no hope for the future ...

"But blessed are those who trust in the LORD and have made the LORD their hope and confidence. They are like trees planted along a riverbank, with roots that reach deep into the water. Such trees are not bothered by the heat or worried by long months of drought. Their leaves stay green, and they never stop producing fruit." (Jeremiah 17:5–8 NLT)

1. According to Jeremiah 17:5–8, what will you look like if you try to handle life's troubles on your own?

2. According to today's passage, what will you look like if you trust in the Lord and make Him your hope and confidence?

"I believed in God, but I didn't have a relationship with Him." –Susan

3. In this life, with all its trials and hurts, where is the most secure place you can choose to run to, again and again?

CONSIDER THIS

Surrender means to yield control or power to someone or something else; it means to give up something in favor of another choice. Surrender enables you to let go of things you are holding too tightly and to accept an even better option. Surrender frees you to be able to hope again.

"You will only find peace through surrender." –Sharon

TALKING TO GOD

God, I need Your help in making this a constant, daily practice. When I'm tempted to fear, or to hold on too tightly to my ideas of what is best, help me to surrender that to You and choose to embrace Your good promises.

DAY 2 | **Making spiritual investments**
What used to be important to you before your loved one's death might not be so important anymore. What does God say to value as you move forward in life?

GOD'S MESSAGE TO YOU
"Don't store up treasures here on earth, where moths eat them and rust destroys them, and where thieves break in and steal. Store your treasures in heaven, where moths and rust cannot destroy, and thieves do not break in and steal. Wherever your treasure is, there the desires of your heart will also be." (Matthew 6:19–21 NLT)

"Turn my eyes away from worthless things." (Psalm 119:37a)

1. What do you treasure/value more now than you did before your loved one's death?

2. What do you place less value on now?

3. Why do you think you need to ask God to help you turn your attention from things that are worthless?

CONSIDER THIS

Sabrina D. Black shares how her values have changed since the death of her loved ones:

- *I tell people I love them more often.*
- *I make more frequent phone calls.*
- *I try to keep short accounts.*
- *I try to be present with people, not thinking about where I need to be or what I need to do next, because I realize those moments are precious.*

"If I didn't have anything, as long as I had Christ, I'd still have everything." –Jodi

TALKING TO GOD

Lord, I want to value You more. I understand now that what matters is eternity. Give me a greater understanding of Your worth. Please turn my eyes from worthless things. Help me to spend increasingly more time doing things that have eternal value.

DAY 3 | **Drenching yourself in the Word**
Spend a lot of time thinking about what the Bible says. That's the key to moving forward.

"I may be hurting, but I'm so much more joyful." –Susan

GOD'S MESSAGE TO YOU

"Oh, the joys of those who ... delight in the law of the LORD [God's words in the Bible], meditating on it day and night. They are like trees planted along the riverbank, bearing fruit each season. Their leaves never wither, and they prosper in all they do." (Psalm 1:1–3 NLT)

1. According to Psalm 1:1–3, who experiences joy?

2. Meditating on God's Word involves an intentional, internal conversation and reflection on the truths you are reading. How often does God say we are to meditate on His Word (see Psalm 1:1–3)?

3. What is the result of meditating on God's Word (see Psalm 1:1–3)?

CONSIDER THIS

"I guarantee if you spend your time in the Word of God, and there's an attitude of yieldedness and surrender to those truths, there'll be power in your life that you never even thought was available."
–Dr. Crawford Loritts

TALKING TO GOD

God, help me to discipline myself not only to read Your Word, but also to think about it, study it, discuss it, and live it. Thank you, God, that there is power in Your Word available to strengthen and encourage me in moving forward in my new normal.

DAY 4

Peace and pain can coexist

In a world filled with suffering, God wants you to learn to experience peace in the midst of difficult situations.

GOD'S MESSAGE TO YOU

"LORD, how many are my foes! ... I call out to the LORD, and he answers me from his holy mountain. I lie down and sleep; I wake again, because the LORD sustains me. I will not fear though tens of thousands assail me on every side." (Psalm 3:1a, 4–6)

1. Instead of focusing on his problem, his many enemies, the writer of Psalm 3 calls out to the Lord for help. When you face difficulties, are you more inclined to focus only on the details of your situation, or do you assess your situation and call out to God?

2. Notice that the psalmist was not ignorant about the details of his dilemma. He knew he had many foes. What do you learn from this example of a godly person who has a clear understanding of the challenges he's facing?

3. Notice the psalmist was able to rest in the midst of a difficult situation. Based on Psalm 3:1a, 4–6, why do you think he was able to experience peace and rest in the midst of difficulty?

CONSIDER THIS

"Not too long after Suzan died, we were in Washington for an event. One morning we had slept a little late, and as we were walking toward the elevator,

---

"It's easier to sit on the couch and have a relationship with the couch than to go out and have relationships with others." –Susan

I blurted out, 'I wonder where Suzan is and what she's doing.' Then it hit me like a ton of bricks. I knew exactly where she was and what she was doing. That was one of those epiphany moments." –Zig Ziglar

TALKING TO GOD

God, I realize my goal isn't to get rid of the pain. Life on earth is painful, but life lived in You brings joy and peace. Help me understand what it looks like to have joy and peace amid my grief.

DAY 5 — Renewing your strength

Hoping in the Lord is the basis of strength, not hoping in different circumstances. Make "hoping in the Lord" a daily practice and discipline in your life in order to renew your strength. How?

Be intentional about:

1. Turning to Him.
2. Letting go of self-reliance to rely instead on Him.
3. Trusting in what the Bible reveals about His character and what He has promised.

GOD'S MESSAGE TO YOU

"He gives strength to the weary and increases the power of the weak. Even youths grow tired and weary, and young men stumble and fall; but those who hope in the LORD will renew their strength. They will soar on wings like eagles; they will run and not grow weary, they will walk and not be faint." (Isaiah 40:29–31)

1. According to Isaiah 40:29–31, how do you know that you can't be strong all the time?

2. According to Isaiah 40:29–31, what is the result of hoping in the Lord?

3. Which part of Isaiah 40:29–31 do you find most encouraging?

CONSIDER THIS

"It was a tough journey. It was painful and hard. But with God's help, I got through it and I'm on the other side. Now I can use what I've learned that is so invaluable. I'd rather have learned it without all the pain and the hurt. But it's worth it now because I can live life more fully, and I have more assurance and peace, and I feel like I can do a whole lot more than what I ever thought I could before."
–Dr. Susan Zonnebelt-Smeenge

TALKING TO GOD

God, You are the source of hope. At times when I feel too weak to move forward, please remind me of who You are, what You've done for me, and how You will help me in that very moment. Refresh and renew my strength as I seek to take steps forward, following Your purposes for my life.

SUSAN: LOOKING BACK

"All these painful paths we go down, God is giving us tools to work with. We can either leave them on the path or we can pick them up and carry them with us. If we carry them with us, then we can pass them to other people and help them along the way. My [original] plan would have gotten us nowhere. I would have been happy just to be what I was. But I wasn't benefiting anybody but my family and myself, and that's not what I'm here for."

Congratulations on completing the GriefShare program! Please consider attending another thirteen-week cycle to further aid your healing. You will also be better able to help other people who have begun the grief process. Other suggestions for what you can do next are found on page 132.

"When I'm in a really hard place, I need some big promises." –Sandy Elder

MY WEEKLY GRIEF WORK

Session - Thirteen

PERSONAL CHECKUP – TRACK YOUR HEALING PROGRESS

Place a check in the box identifying how you're feeling. Insert words to explain why.

	REALLY BAD	OKAY	PRETTY GOOD	GREAT
EMOTIONALLY				
PHYSICALLY				
SPIRITUALLY				
RELATIONALLY				

JOURNAL TOPICS – MAKING SENSE OF IT ALL

Choose the idea below, or choose your own topic. We encourage
you to use a separate notebook for your weekly journaling.

✎ Talk to God about the fears you have about reengaging in life and moving forward. Ask for His help in surrendering those fears to Him.

MOVING FORWARD – PRACTICAL STEPS TOWARD HEALING
HOW TO CREATE A NEW NORMAL AND MOVE FORWARD

First, ask yourself these questions; then, prayerfully take steps to put what you've learned into practice.*

1. What things am I passionate about?

2. What has God given me a burden for?

3. What skills and talents has God given me that I could use?

4. What life experiences have I been through that God might be able to redeem or utilize?

5. How could these talents, abilities, passions, and my personality come together in the life of my local church?

* These questions were shared by GriefShare expert Brad Hambrick.

WHAT'S NEXT ?

As this thirteen-week GriefShare journey ends, you'll find you've discovered new concepts and have made precious friendships. You might be eager to put into practice what you've learned, but might also desire further teaching and continued support. Here are suggestions to help you grow and develop.

REPEAT GRIEFSHARE

By repeating another thirteen-week cycle, you will catch things you missed the first time around, and you'll be sure to gain new insights because you will be at a different level of growth. You will also continue to refine the helpful strategies that you've only recently put into practice. Additionally, you can encourage first-time group members, and you'll enjoy the continued friendships of others on their healing journey.

CONNECT WITH ANOTHER CHURCH FELLOWSHIP/STUDY GROUP

Consider joining a Bible study group or another small group sponsored by this church or your home church. Your group leaders can give you more information on what's offered here and the groups that would be most beneficial to you. You'll find that a lot of support and encouragement is available if you take the first step.

KEEP UP SUPPORTIVE RELATIONSHIPS

You will also benefit from continued same-sex friendships with people in your GriefShare group. Plan family get-togethers, regularly meet for coffee, keep in touch via phone and computer. Choose people who will pray with you, encourage you, hold you accountable, and help you grow closer to the Lord– and do the same for them!

GAIN DEEPER INSIGHTS INTO SOME OF THE TOPICS YOU'VE LEARNED

Flip back to the Resource Center on page x. This page directs you to other resources that will help you go deeper as you continue your healing journey.

HELP OTHERS GRIEVING THE DEATH OF A LOVED ONE

Some of you might have interest in helping others in grief. If you are mature and healed, there may be an opportunity for you to become part of the leadership team of this GriefShare program. Talk with your group leaders if you are interested in exploring this idea.

MyGriefShare+

Your group is ending but your healing has just begun

Your personal GriefShare video library

$25 annual subscription

Continue healing with GriefShare's new video streaming service

Just because your group is coming to a close doesn't mean your healing has to. Subscribe today to MyGriefShare+ to access a personal library of hundreds of GriefShare videos.

With this annual subscription service, you can:

- Access 200+ videos essential to your healing
- Get more advice from popular GriefShare experts & testimonials
- Find answers to the questions you have about your grief
- Learn more about your grief by watching previous editions of GriefShare

NEW CONTENT ADDED MONTHLY

Subscribe today!

GRIEFSHARE.ORG/PLUS

NOTES NOTES

NOTES

THANK YOU AND INVITATION CARDS

Express your appreciation to the sponsors of your GriefShare program. Share your comments on the card below with your group leaders and the pastor of the church that sponsors your group.

Use the other cards to invite people to attend GriefShare.

THANK YOU!

I have been a participant in the GriefShare program sponsored by this church. Through this card, I want to share my comments and let you know how the program has helped me during this difficult time.

Comments _____

_____

How GriefShare has helped me _____

_____

_____

Name (optional) _____ GRIEF SHARE

(Additional comments on reverse side)

YOUR JOURNEY FROM MOURNING TO JOY

Find help after the death of a loved one at GriefShare, a special seminar/support group designed to help you heal from the deep loss you have experienced. It's helped me a lot.

Why not come to our next meeting?

Day _____

Time _____

Place _____

Address _____

Email _____ GRIEF SHARE

Phone _____

YOUR JOURNEY FROM MOURNING TO JOY

Find help after the death of a loved one at GriefShare, a special seminar/support group designed to help you heal from the deep loss you have experienced. It's helped me a lot.

Why not come to our next meeting?

Day _____

Time _____

Place _____

Address _____

Email _____ GRIEF SHARE

Phone _____

BOOKMARK

YOUR
JOURNEY
FROM MOURNING
TO **JOY**

GRIEF SHARE

A Ministry of Church Initiative
P.O. Box 1739, Wake Forest, NC 27588
919-562-2112
info@griefshare.org

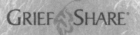

www.griefshare.org

YOUR
JOURNEY
FROM MOURNING
TO JOY

"FOR I [GOD]
WILL TURN THEIR
MOURNING INTO
JOY AND WILL
COMFORT THEM
AND GIVE THEM
JOY FOR THEIR
SORROW."

**JEREMIAH
31:13 NASB**

THANK YOU AND INVITATION CARDS

Express your appreciation to the sponsors of your GriefShare program. Share your comments on the card below with your group leaders and the pastor of the church that sponsors your group.

Use the other cards to invite people to attend GriefShare.

PLEASE FORWARD THIS CARD TO:

Group leaders _____

Pastor _____

Other _____

_____

Additional comments _____

_____

_____

_____

_____

_____

"FOR I [GOD] WILL TURN THEIR MOURNING INTO JOY
AND WILL COMFORT THEM AND GIVE THEM
JOY FOR THEIR SORROW."

JEREMIAH 31:13 NASB

"FOR I [GOD] WILL TURN THEIR MOURNING INTO JOY
AND WILL COMFORT THEM AND GIVE THEM
JOY FOR THEIR SORROW."

JEREMIAH 31:13 NASB